IRAN IN LATIN AMERICA: THREAT OR 'AXIS OF ANNOYANCE'?

Latin American Program
Middle East Program

IRAN IN LATIN AMERICA: THREAT OR 'AXIS OF ANNOYANCE'?

Edited by
Cynthia Arnson, Haleh Esfandiari and Adam Stubits

Woodrow Wilson Center Reports on the Americas # 23

Available from the Latin American Program

Woodrow Wilson International Center for Scholars
One Woodrow Wilson Plaza
1300 Pennsylvania Avenue NW
Washington, DC 20004-3027

www.wilsoncenter.org/lap

ISBN 1-933549-95-5

The photograph on the cover of this publication was taken on June 10, 2007, during a speech by Nicaraguan President Daniel Ortega to students at Tehran University. An Iranian student is holding a sign which adjoins portraits of Presidents Hugo Chávez (Venezuela), Mahmoud Ahmadinejad (Iran), Fidel Castro (Cuba), Daniel Ortega (Nicaragua) and Evo Morales (Bolivia), emblazoned with the words "Alliance for Justice." Notably, the words are written not in Farsi or in Spanish, as one might expect, but rather, in English, apparently for an audience in the United States.
Photo: Getty Images

The Woodrow Wilson International Center for Scholars is the national, living memorial honoring President Woodrow Wilson. In providing an essential link between the worlds of ideas and public policy, the Center addresses current and emerging challenges confronting the United States and the world. The Center promotes policy-relevant research and dialogue to increase understanding and enhance the capabilities and knowledge of leaders, citizens, and institutions worldwide. Created by an Act of Congress in 1968, the Center is a nonpartisan institution headquartered in Washington, D.C., and supported by both public and private funds.

CONTENTS

PREFACE

As this publication goes to press, Iran's relationship with Latin America has once again captured headlines. Iranian President Mahmoud Ahmadinejad made a state visit to Brazil in late November 2009, the first Iranian president to have done so since the mid-1960s. During the visit, Brazilian President Luiz Inácio Lula da Silva publicly defended Iran's right to develop nuclear energy for peaceful purposes, and portrayed the invitation to Ahmadinejad as part of a Brazilian effort to play a broader role in brokering peace in the Middle East. Indeed, Ahmadinejad's visit followed closely upon visits to Brasília by both Israeli President Shimon Peres and Palestinian Authority President Mahmoud Abbas.

Lula's diplomatic overture to the Iranian leader elicited sharp criticism both in Brazil and the United States. Critics pointed to Iran's continued defiance of the international community over access to its nuclear facilities by the International Atomic Energy Agency as well as the Iranian government's stepped up repression of domestic opponents following disputed presidential elections in June 2009. Before returning to Tehran, Ahmadinejad also went to Bolivia and made his fourth visit to Venezuela. In Caracas, President Hugo Chávez welcomed the Iranian president as a "gladiator of anti-imperialist struggles" and used the occasion to denounce Israel as "the murderous arm of the Yankee empire.[1]

As this report demonstrates, the growing and multi-layered relationship between Iran and numerous Latin American countries since Ahmadinejad's election in 2005 is driven by a combination of factors. These include, for both sides, and economic self-interest, shared anti-U.S. and anti-imperialist ideology, and the desire—especially evident in the Brazilian case—to play a larger role on the world stage, assert foreign policy independence, and diversify international partners beyond the United States. However, of special concern to the international community is the nature of Iran's intentions regarding its nuclear program and what they might portend for Iran's relationship with countries of the Western hemisphere.

The economic relationship between Iran and Latin America is growing although its full extent is hard to quantify. There is not only a lack of reliable statistics but also a vast chasm between the promise and actual realization of productive and infrastructure investments by Iran. International Monetary Fund figures compiled by the *Latin Business Chronicle* indicate that trade between Iran and Latin America tripled between 2007 and 2008, rising to $2.9 billion—almost half of which was between Brazil and Iran. (By these estimates Venezuela, whose relationship with Iran has raised the greatest amount of political and strategic concern, is in fifth place, behind Argentina, Ecuador, and Peru.[2]) By contrast, total trade between China and Latin America in the same 2007-2008 period amounted to $140 billion, an amount that dwarfs the trade between the region and Iran.[3]

Moreover, while political and commercial relations are closely correlated, they are not always identical. Argentina is Iran's second largest trading partner in Latin America, yet its diplomatic relationship is deeply strained. Argentina has asked for the extradition of several current and former Iranian government officials for their roles in the terrorist bombing of a Jewish community center in Buenos Aires. In September 2009, and under instruction from Argentine President Cristina Fernández de Kirchner, the Argentine delegation walked out of the room when President Ahmadinejad began to address the UN General Assembly.[4]

Iran's behavior in the international system, from its support of terrorist movements, to the limited cooperation with international inspections of its nuclear program, has logically raised concern and even alarm about its increased activities in Latin America. The Manhattan District Attorney's office has launched an ongoing investigation of Venezuelan collaboration with Iran to procure financing and materials (including uranium) for weapons production in violation of U.S. and international sanctions.[5] Some analysts have gone so far as to claim that that Venezuela's "encouragement of the penetration of the Western Hemisphere by the Islamic Republic of Iran" constitutes a strategic threat to U.S. national security and that of the Western Hemisphere.[6] Others have called on the Obama administration to "confront the grave threat posed by Chávez."[7] Within the U.S. government, however, there is divided opinion over how to interpret Iran's increased involvement in Latin America and the danger it poses.

The essays in this report reflect an effort to provide background and context for understanding Iran's relations with Argentina, Bolivia, Ecuador,

Nicaragua, and Venezuela; the articles emphasize the foreign policy objectives and strategies of Latin American nations as well as the strategic objectives of the Iranian government. Originally presented at a conference at the Woodrow Wilson Center in July 2008, the papers have been revised, translated, and updated since. We make no claim to having the final word on this controversial and ever-changing subject. Indeed, the lack of transparency in many aspects of the Iranian-Latin American relationship, and particularly, the clandestine nature of many of the alleged activities, point to the need for additional, dispassionate analysis. In calling for additional research, we emphasize the need for facts to serve as the drivers of policy, not the other way around. That this has not always been the case, especially in the recent past, should make us all doubly careful.

Cynthia J. Arnson, *Director, Latin American Program*
Haleh Esfandiari, *Director, Middle East Program*

Notes

1 Quoted in Simon Romero, "In Welcoming Iranian President, Chávez Blasts Israel," *New York Times*, November 26, 2009, p. 12. See also, "Ayatollahs in the Backyard," *Economist*, November 8-December 4, 2009, p. 41.

2 "Latin America: Iran Trade Triples," *Latin Business Chronicle*, December 2, 2009.

3 "China-Latin American Trade: New Record," *Latin Business Chronicle*, November 23, 2009.

4 Letter to Cynthia Arnson from Argentine Ambassador Héctor Timerman, September 30, 2009.

5 "The Link between Iran and Venezuela: A Crisis in the Making?" Briefing by Robert M. Morgenthau at the Brookings Institution, Washington, D.C., September 8, 2009.

6 Norman A. Bailey, "Iranian Penetration into the Western Hemisphere through Venezuela," Remarks prepared for presentation at the Kingston Conference on International Security, June 2009, mimeo, p. 1. According to Bailey, Iranian activities and installations in Venezuela "are designed to facilitate and provide cover for illegal and subversive endeavors that not only involve the Iranian government but also terrorist organizations such as Hamas, Hezbollah, Islamic Jihad, the Colombian FARC and drug cartels from Colombia, Mexico and Venezuela."

7 Roger F. Noriega, "Hugo Chávez's Criminal Nuclear Network: A Grave and Growing Threat," American Enterprise Institute, *Latin American Outlook*, No. 3, October 2009.

INTRODUCTION

ADAM STUBITS

On December 2, 1823, President James Monroe, in his State of the Union Address, established the principles of what is now known as the Monroe Doctrine: that the United States would consider any nation's attempt to extend "their system to any portion of this hemisphere as dangerous to our peace and safety."[1] Nearly two hundred years later, President George W. Bush, in his 2002 State of the Union Address, included the Islamic Republic of Iran in his now famous "axis of evil," emphasizing it was "arming to threaten the peace of the world."[2] It is therefore not surprising that the developing economic and political relations between the Iranian government and the governments of Bolivia, Ecuador, and Nicaragua—in addition to the more long-term relationship with Venezuela—have raised concerns in both the United States and the region about Iranian objectives in Latin America.

Iran's involvement in Latin America is unquestionable, and is growing at a rapid pace; within four years of President Mahmoud Ahmadinejad being elected in 2005, Iran opened six new embassies in Latin America including Bolivia, Chile, Colombia, Ecuador, Nicaragua, and Uruguay, in addition to the five embassies already in operation – Argentina, Brazil, Cuba, Mexico and Venezuela.[3] Indeed, in no uncertain terms, Ahmadinejad has declared, "When the Western countries were trying to isolate Iran, we went to the U.S. backyard."[4] Throughout the region, Iran is brokering potentially significant economic deals. Iran and Venezuela have entered into more than two hundred bilateral agreements on a variety of issues[5] while Ecuador and Iran have entered into an energy cooperation deal that calls for cooperation in the building of an energy refinery and petrochemical unit in Ecuador, training of Ecuadorian oil sector workers by Iranian experts and assistance with maintenance of Ecuadorian facilities.[6] In Nicaragua, Ahmadinejad has pledged to rebuild a sea port on Monkey Bay at a cost of more than $350 million.[7] In addition, Bolivia has been promised Iranian investments of more than $1 billion over the next five years[8]. In August 2009, Iran "offered Bolivia a loan of $280 million, in addition to spending $200 million on building two cement factories and three milk facilities." [9] These numbers and others frequently reported are agreements and do not represent actual investments or expenditures on the part of the Iranian government. Farideh Farhi, has noted that Ahmadinejad "can go around and sign all these things, but ultimately it's the Iranian parliament that has to decide whether it's going to" fund each specific initiative.[10] Between 2001 and 2007, Iran and Venezuela entered into 180 cooperative agreements, valued by Iran at $20 billion. Nevertheless, the International Monetary Fund estimated their bilateral trade at just $16 million in fiscal year 2006.

While Iran is clearly driving the relationship, Latin America is far more than a passive participant observer. Following Iran's commitment to invest $1.1 billion in Bolivia's gas facilities, Bolivian President Evo Morales declared that the country's only embassy in the Middle East would move from Cairo to Tehran. More significantly, Morales lifted longstanding visa restrictions, allowing anyone with an Iranian passport to enter Bolivia without a visa or other documentation.[11] Morales' plea on *The Daily Show*, "Please don't consider me part of the axis of evil,"[12] notwithstanding, he has cautioned, "We will never promote war but nor do we accept that in the name of peace the criteria of the strongest prevails."[13] Hugo Chávez's decision to allow the establishment of Iran's Banco Internacional de Desarrollo (BID) in Caracas provided Iran with a "foothold into the Venezuelan banking system" , "a perfect 'sanctions-busting' method," allowing Iran to evade U.S. financial sanctions.[14]

Allegations abound, however, that Iran's economic interests in Latin America are secondary, or at worst a cover, for more sinister desires. In November 2008, Turkish customs officials seized a suspicious Iranian shipment bound for Venezuela. The shipment, manifested as "tractor parts," actually contained barrels of nitrate and sulfite chemicals, commonly used for explosives, as well as dismantled laboratory equipment. Turkish officials engaged their Office of Atomic Energy and military experts to examine the materials.[15] Similarly, some doubt the legitimacy of the plants and factories constructed by Iran in Venezuela. Robert Morgenthau, District Attorney for New York County, has suggested, "we should be concerned that illegal activity might be taking place" because of their "remote" location and "secretive nature."[16] Nevertheless, on both sides, there exists a disconnect between pledges of cooperation and realities on the ground. U.S. Secretary of State Hilary Rodham Clinton commented, for example, "The Iranians are building a huge embassy in Managua," concluding, "and you can only imagine what that's for."[17] Not only did the Nicaraguan and Iranian governments deny such a project, but even a U.S. diplomat in Managua admitted, "There is no huge Iranian Embassy being built as far as we can tell." A U.S. State Department spokesperson concluded, "It perhaps suggests the Iranians are talking about investments and influence that they don't yet have."[18]

Given Iran's nuclear capabilities, there is concern throughout the region and in the United States as to what role supportive countries like Venezuela might play in the advancement and proliferation of nuclear technologies. Colombian President Álvaro Uribe has expressed concern saying, "We are very worried and I can't refrain from saying so, that nuclear war be brought to our neighborhood. This is very serious, very worrying,"[19] and with seemingly good reason. In September 2009, "Iran said it test-fired short-range missiles, just days after it confirmed it is building a second uranium-enrichment facility."[20] Rodolfo Sanz, Venezuela's minister of basic industries and mining has indicated that Venezuela "could have important reserves of Uranium," and while he rejects allegations that Venezuela is supplying Iran's nuclear program, he did confirm that "Iran is helping us with geophysical aerial probes and geochemical analyses."[21] In September 2009, Chávez announced an agreement with Russia for assistance in developing a nuclear energy program and plans for the establishment of a "nuclear village" with technological assistance from Iran.[22]

Asked if Washington is worried, Thomas Shannon, then the top State Department official for Latin America, responded, "What worries us is Iran's history of activities in the region and especially its links to Hezbollah and the terrorist attacks that took place in Buenos Aires," concluding, "Past is prologue."[23] As far back as November 2007, the United States House of Representatives passed a resolution "expressing concern about threats to the U.S. by deepening economic and security ties between Iran and like-minded regimes in the Western Hemisphere, including Venezuela." The resolution had its base in "evidence that Iranian-backed Hezbollah, a designated terrorist organization, raises millions from counterfeit products produced in the tri-border region of Brazil, Paraguay, and Argentina, and growing efforts backed by Iran to foment anti-Americanism and anti-Semitism."[24] It is therefore no surprise that in 2008, the U.S. Treasury Department accused the Chávez government of "employing and providing safe harbor to Hezbollah facilitators and fundraisers." [25] In a hearing before the Senate Armed Services Committee, Navy Admiral James Stavridis, then Commander of the U.S. Southern Command, testified that "We have seen... an increase in a wide level of activity by the Iranian government in this region." He continued, "That is a concern principally because of the connections between the government of Iran, which is a state sponsor of terrorism, and Hezbollah."[26] It is relevant to note that at the printing of this publication, there is global controversy over Ahmadinejad's nomination of Ahmad Vahidi as the minister of defense for Iran. Vahidi is one of five Iranian officials wanted by Interpol to face charges in Argentina for alleged involvement in the 1994 bombing of a Jewish cultural center in Buenos Aires.[27] Without providing any specifics, Stavridis also testified, "We have been seeing in Colombia a direct connection between Hezbollah activity and narco-trafficking activity."[28] In October 2008, following a two-year investigation, 36 suspects were arrested in Colombia on charges related to cocaine smuggling and money laundering. Gladys Sanchez, the lead investigator for the case said, "The profits from the sales of drugs went to finance Hezbollah. This is an example of how narco-trafficking is a theme of interest to all criminal organizations, the FARC, the paramilitaries and terrorists." [29]

In July 2008, with the goal of providing a balanced and dispassionate overview of Iran's relations with Bolivia, Ecuador, Nicaragua, and Venezuela, the Woodrow Wilson International Center for Scholars' Latin American Program and Middle East Program convened a conference to examine the foreign policy objectives and strategies of these Latin American nations as well as the strategic objectives of the Iranian government. Additionally, the conference aimed to explore allegations of Iranian involvement in the bombings of the Jewish community center (AMIA) and the Israeli Embassy in Buenos Aires. Specialists on Bolivia, Ecuador, Nicaragua, Venezuela, and Iran were asked to address some of the following questions: aside from the symbolism of Iranian President Ahmadinejad's presence at various presidential inaugurations in the region, what kind of assistance has been provided? What lies in the realm of promises (investments, subsidized oil, etc.) but has yet to materialize? What, if any, concrete initiatives are underway? Aside from growing economic and political ties, are there indications of military or intelligence cooperation? Rhetoric and photo opportunities aside, what is the substance of Iran's relationships with countries in the hemisphere?

Douglas Farah, president of IBI Consultants and a Senior Fellow at the International Assessment and Strategy Center asserts that Iran's broadening presence in Latin America is promoted by the unwavering relationship between Hugo Chávez and Mahmoud Ahmadinejad, necessitated by Iran's search for international political support, and fortified by anti-imperialist attitudes toward the United States. As the dominant oil provider in the region, Venezuela connects Latin American countries, including Ecuador and Nicaragua, to Iran and facilitates their collaboration. Moreover, Iran's diplomatic expansion into countries such as Argentina, Mexico, and Colombia reflect Ahmadinejad's intentions to bolster political support amid international condemnation and sanctions in forums such as the Security Council and European Union. Farah clarifies that Iran's relationship with Latin America is primarily political, not economic, given that most Latin American trade with the United States vastly outweighs commerce with Iran. Finally, mutual antagonism toward the United States unites Iran and some Latin American countries. The existence of a common enemy and the recognition that the United States has largely excluded Latin America from its post 9/11 agenda has forged their partnership and has created an opening for Iran to fill.

Farah also expresses concern about the lack of transparency in the Iranian-Latin American alignment. Not only is there an inability to track Iranian aid delivered to Nicaragua, Bolivia, and Ecuador, but more distressing is the creation of the Venezuela Banco Internacional de Desarrollo (BID) and the Banco Binacional Iraní-Venezolano; their heavy Iranian investment and leadership signal the evasion of international sanctions previously imposed on Iranian banking institutions. Moreover, no records exist for the direct flights between Caracas and Tehran, returning through Damascus. Farah suggests further examination of these flights, as Iran and Venezuela have relatively weak commercial and tourist ties and travel to either country does not require visas.

Farideh Farhi, former Public Policy Scholar at the Woodrow Wilson Center and Adjunct Professor of Political Science at the University of Hawaii, argues that while Iran's increased attention to Latin America as a region is a relatively new development, its bilateral ties with some individual Latin American nations are long-standing and relatively robust. Iran has shared an ideological relationship with Cuba since the end of the Iran-Iraq War, and a political relationship with Venezuela since their co-founding of OPEC in the 1960s. The impetus behind these long-standing bilateral relationships is three-fold: First, Iran's non-aligned position in foreign policy has compelled it to seek out countries with similar ideological outlooks. Second, determined efforts by the United States at keeping Iran in diplomatic and economic isolation have forced it to pursue an active foreign policy. Finally, the election of a reformist president in 1997 made it possible for countries like Brazil to engage Iran with enough confidence to withstand pressures from the United States.

Since Mahmoud Ahmadinejad's 2005 election to the presidency, however, Tehran's relations with Latin America have become highly publicized and have focused on mutual opposition to U.S. policies. Relations with Venezuela are touted as a "poke in the eye" to the United States, with the hope of producing economic benefits, influence (for Iran and Venezuela), and angst (for the United States). Iran has also sought highly publicized relationships with Bolivia, Nicaragua, and Ecuador, promising lucrative investments, including, for example, a $350 million deepwater seaport off Nicaragua's Atlantic coast, and a "dry canal" of pipelines, rails, and highways across the country. Farhi argues, however, that the new-found intensity of these relationships is unsustainable. The recent iteration of Iran's relations in Latin America is based on political opportunism, as a diplomatic thorn in America's side, rather than a more long-term economic or military partnership. Already, the proposed deepwater seaport is facing resistance in Nicaragua by land right activists. Iran's real commitment to this project is also not clear and Tehran has so far refused to forgo Nicaragua's $152 million debt, despite Ortega's specific request that it do so. Ultimately, Farhi predicts that while bilateral relations between Iran and individual Latin American countries will continue to gradually improve, based on economic give and take and a degree of shared commitment to non-alignment, the intensely vitriolic character of current relations would not continue past Ahmadinejad's term in office.

Elodie Brun of the Institut d'Études Politiques, Paris, notes that Iran and Venezuela are, respectively, the second and fourth largest oil producers in OPEC. Although the historical relationship between the two countries stretches back over many decades, relations have intensified since the election of President Ahmadinejad in 2005. Between 2005 and 2007, each president visited the other's country three times and commercial relations have vastly expanded: trade, which amounted to $1.1 million in 2004, grew to $50.7 million in 2006. According to Brun, both countries are benefiting from—and promoting--high oil rents, using oil as a political instrument to insert themselves internationally in a way that both characterize as revolutionary. Venezuelan President Hugo Chávez and President Ahmadinejad embrace a rhetoric emphasizing autonomy and independence from the great powers, primarily the United States but also Europe, citing unity in the struggle against imperialism and capitalism. Hostility to the United States, and particularly to the administration of George W. Bush, is what most binds the foreign policies of the two countries together. Brun argued that Chávez has served as Ahmadinejad's "port of entry" into Latin America, reinforcing Chávez's own leadership role while helping Iran step out of its international isolation. Venezuela has helped forge relationships with Venezuelan allies such as Bolivia, Ecuador, and Nicaragua and has also defended Iran's nuclear ambitions.

Beyond the political realm, Venezuela has turned to Iran as a source of investment for infrastructure and industrial development, including in the oil and petrochemicals sectors. A large gap, nonetheless, separates the signing and actual implementation of cooperation agreements, and coming years will demonstrate whether many of the proposed projects are viable, particularly if oil income declines from its current high.

Hugo Alconada Mon, former Washington correspondent of the Argentine daily *La Nación*, cites evidence linking groups affiliated with Hezbollah, a Lebanese fundamentalist group, to the terrorist bombings of the Israeli Embassy in Buenos Aires in 1992 and of the AMIA Jewish community center in 1994. Investigations by Argentine judicial authorities have concluded that the attacks were masterminded and orchestrated by Hezbollah with Iranian backing. The U.S. and Israeli governments have also alleged Iranian involvement in the attacks. Although investigations have been ongoing, no one involved in either of the attacks has been brought to justice, and the court cases have been marred by improprieties. One Argentine federal judge overseeing the AMIA investigation was impeached and removed from his post for gross irregularities, including the falsification of evidence. Two other federal prosecutors dropped the case and all three are currently under investigation for the cover up of evidence. The Iranian government has insisted that judicial corruption in Argentina, not Iran's lack of cooperation, accounts for the failure to arrest the masterminds of the attack, and has accused "Zionist lobbies" of making unfounded accusations against Iran. Lebanon's ambassador to Argentina has called Hezbollah's participation in the AMIA attack a theory reinforced "by the political motivation of Israel and the United States."

In May 2006, the Argentine Supreme Court annulled the findings of the lower courts, criticizing the inefficiency of Argentina's intelligence services and the lack of legal bodies to investigate terrorism cases. The Court reaffirmed, nonetheless, the allegations of Iranian involvement and called for the arrest of 14 current and former Iranian government officials. Other arrest warrants have been issued for former President Carlos Menem as well as senior Argentine intelligence and police officials for their alleged role in covering up evidence in the AMIA case and protecting those responsible. In 2007 Interpol approved orders for the arrest of five Iranian officials and a Lebanese national. Former Argentine President Néstor Kirchner accused Iran of failing to fully cooperate with the Argentine judicial authorities.

Javier Meléndez and Félix Maradiaga, from the Institute of Strategic Studies and Public Policies (IEEPP) in Nicaragua, discuss the underpinnings of recent agreements between Iranian President Mahmoud Ahmadinejad and Nicaraguan President Daniel Ortega. According to Maradiaga, Nicaragua's foreign policy strongly correlates with Venezuela's, and any Latin American relationship with Iran is conducted through Caracas. Both Ahmadinejad and Ortega made state visits to each other's countries, resulting in Iranian promises of some $1 billion in aid and investment. The funds are to be used to develop the energy and agricultural sectors, infrastructure, and water purification in Nicaragua. The largest project establishes a deep-water port on Nicaragua's eastern shores, which would require an investment of $350 million. The proposed projects create the appearance of strong economic ties between the two nations. However, Meléndez and Maradiaga state that there was little evidence that the aid and investment would materialize. He doubted that the relationship-- held together by the anti-Americanism espoused by leaders of both countries--would deepen beyond the ideological and political level.

César Montúfar of the Universidad Andina Simón Bolívar in Quito, Ecuador, discusses diplomatic and commercial ties between Ecuador and Iran. Prior to 2007, ties were minimal, and neither country had diplomatic or commercial offices in the capital of the other. Trade has been minimal; in 2000, 2006, and 2007, no Ecuadorian exports reached Iran, and in 2003, the year of highest trade, Ecuador's total exports to Iran valued $ 2.5 million. Montúfar stated that Ahmadinejad's short and surprising visit to Rafael Correa's presidential inauguration spawned a new and short-lived bilateral relationship between the two countries. Correa maintained that the relationship was not political but based solely on commercial interests. There is little evidence of a growing commercial relationship between Quito and Tehran. According to Montúfar, the ties between Ecuador and Iran were established because of Ecuador's relationship with Venezuela. Nevertheless, Montúfar argued, Venezuela's influence in Ecuador is declining, which has been followed by similar decreases in the Iran-Ecuador relationship.

Gustavo Fernández, former Foreign Minister of Bolivia, emphasized the two-fold nature of Bolivia's foreign policy strategy. The first part is an historical indigenous-claims movement with President Evo Morales as the central figure and the people as his foundation. As an Indian president presiding over an Indian population, Morales sought to end the historic exploitation and exclusion of indigenous groups. Initially, countries with indigenous populations, such as Peru and Guatemala, lauded his efforts, and after, resented his encroachment on their domestic policies. According to Fernández, revolution, anti-imperialism, and socialism also characterize Bolivian foreign policy; the nationalization of the oil and telecommunications sectors and the expulsion of the U.S. ambassador reflect this approach. Bolivia has sustained strategic alliances with Cuba and Venezuela, and in South America, with Brazil, Argentina,

Chile, Peru, and Colombia. Their relationships range from friendly to distant and antagonistic.

Fernández claims that the Bolivian-Iranian alignment is more complex. During Ahmadinejad's 2007 visit to La Paz, he and Morales signed a joint declaration recognizing the development of nuclear energy for peaceful purposes and allocating joint funds to utilize other energy sources. They also signed a Memorandum of Understanding to ease the transfer of technology and training and to establish investments. Recent plans include broadcasting Iranian television in the Cochabamba/Chapare region. The author observes that their relationship is mostly political, achieved through a shared anti-U.S. agenda. Their alliance is important geopolitically because Bolivia joins Venezuela, Nicaragua, and Ecuador in the campaign for Venezuelan led regional integration and stricter treatment of foreign investment. Conversely, Peru, Colombia, and Chile desire full integration in the global economy through trade agreements with the United States, the European Union, and APEC. In the international context, Russia's will to reassert itself carries important implications for the United States, Iran, and Latin America.

Notes

1 James Monroe, "Monroe Doctrine; December 2 1823," The Avalon Project, Yale Law Library, Dec. 2, 1823, available at http://avalon.law.yale.edu/19th_century/monroe.asp

2 George W. Bush, Address before a joint session of the Congress on the state of the union, Jan. 29,2002, *Weekly Compilation of Presidential Documents*, 125-172., available at http://frwebgate.access.gpo.gov/cgi-bin/getdoc.cgi?dbname=2002_presidential_documents&docid=pd04fe02_txt-11.

3 Anne-Marie O'Connor and Mary Beth Sheridan, "Iran's Invisible Nicaragua Embassy," *The Washington Post*, Jul. 13, 2009. Available at http://www.washingtonpost.com/wp-dyn/content/article/2009/07/12/ AR2009071202337.html.

4 Román Ortiz, "Ayatollahs cast growing shadow in Latin America," *The Atlanta Journal-Constitution*, Sep. 9, 2009. Available at http://www.ajc.com/opinion/ayatollahs-cast-growing-shadow-135031.html.

5 Kelley Vlahos, "'Axis of Unity' in Latin America Could Be Growing Threat for the U.S.," *Fox News*, Mar. 4, 2008. Available at http://www.foxnews.com/story/0,2933,330488,00.html.

6 "Iran, Ecuador sign deal on energy, refinery plan," *Thomson Financial News*, Sep. 14, 2008. Available at http://www.forbes.com/feeds/afx/2008/09/14/afx5421244.html.

7 Kelley Vlahos, "'Axis of Unity' in Latin America Could Be Growing Threat for the U.S.," *Fox News*, Mar. 4, 2008. Available at http://www.foxnews.com/story/0,2933,330488,00.html.

8 "Morales: Iran, Brazil and Venezuela gas investments could make for Bolivian record in 2008," *International Herald Tribune*, Jan. 3, 2008.

9 "The dragon in the backyard," *The Economist*, Aug. 13, 2009. Available at http://www.economist.com/ displaystory.cfm?story_id=14209932.

10 Anne-Marie O'Connor and Mary Beth Sheridan, "Iran's Invisible Nicaragua Embassy," *The Washington Post*, Jul. 13, 2009. Available at http://www.washingtonpost.com/wp-dyn/content/article/2009/07/12/ AR2009071202337.html.

11 John Kiriakou, "Iran's Latin America Push," *The Los Angeles Times,* Nov. 8, 2008. Available at http://www.latimes.com/news/opinion/la-oe-kiriakou8-2008nov08,0,878526.story.

12 Eduardo Garcia, "Iran's leader courts Latin American leftists," *Reuters*, Sep. 27, 2007. Available at http://www.reuters.com/article/worldNews/idUSN2734139720070927.

13 Rory Carroll, "South America embraces Bush's arch enemy," *The Guardian*, Sep. 29, 2007. Available at http://www.guardian.co.uk/world/2007/sep/29/venezuela.iran.

14 Robert M. Morgenthau, "The Link Between Iran and Venezuela: A Crisis in the Making?" (briefing presented at the Brookings Institution, September 8, 2009).

15 United States Department of State. Office of the Coordinator for Counterterrorism. *Country Reports on Terrorism 2008*, Apr. 2009. Available at http://www.libraries.iub.edu/index.php?pageId=2558.

16 Steve Stecklow and Farnaz Fassihi, "Iran's Global Foray Has Mixed Results," *The Wall Street* Journal, Sep. 29, 2009. Available at http://online.wsj.com/article/SB125409124052344735.html.

17 Anne-Marie O'Connor and Mary Beth Sheridan, "Iran's Invisible Nicaragua Embassy," *The Washington Post*, Jul. 13, 2009. Available at http://www.washingtonpost.com/wp-dyn/content/article/2009/07/12/ AR2009071202337.html.

18 Op.Cit.

19 Andres Openheimer, "Brazil a nuclear power? Probably not," *The Miami Herald*, Oct. 18, 2009. Available at http://www.miamiherald.com/news/columnists/andres-oppenheimer/story/1288046.html.

20 Steve Stecklow and Farnaz Fassihi, "Iran's Global Foray Has Mixed Results," *The Wall Street* Journal, Sep. 29, 2009. Available at http://online.wsj.com/article/SB125409124052344735.html.

21 Simon Romero, "Venezuela Says Iran Is Helping It Look for Uranium," *The New York Times*, Sep. 25, 2009. Available at http://www.nytimes.com/2009/09/26/world/americas/26venez.html.

22 Op. Cit

23 Andres Oppenheimer, "Beware Iran in Latin America," *The Miami Herald*, Sep. 30, 2007.

24 U.S. House of Representatives. House Foreign Affairs Committee, "Ros-Lehtinen Hails Expected Passage of Resolution on Iran's Growing Role in Western Hemisphere," Nov. 5, 2007.

25 Jamie Daremblum, "The Chávez-Iran Alliance: A Menace to the Western Hemisphere," *Real Clear* World, Sep. 21, 2009. Available at http://www.realclearworld.com/articles/2009/09/21/Chávez_iran_alliance_menace_to_western_hemisphere.html.

26 David Morgan, "U.S. says Iran increasing activity in Latin America," *Reuters*, Mar. 17, 2009. Available at http://www.reuters.com/article/worldNews/idUSTRE52G5VK20090317.

27 Michael Slackman, "Ahmadinejad Nominee Is Wanted in '94 Bombing," *The New York Times*, Aug. 21, 2009. Available at http://www.nytimes.com/2009/08/22/world/middleeast/22iran.html?_r=2.

28 David Morgan, "U.S. says Iran increasing activity in Latin America," *Reuters*, Mar. 17, 2009. Available at http://www.reuters.com/article/worldNews/idUSTRE52G5VK20090317.

29 Chris Kraul and Sebastian Rotella, "Colombian cocaine ring linked to Hezbollah," *The Los Angeles Times*, Oct. 22, 2008. Available at http://articles.latimes.com/2008/oct/22/world/fg-cocainering22.

IRAN IN LATIN AMERICA: AN OVERVIEW

Douglas Farah

There is considerable debate over the level of threat posed by Iran's expanding diplomatic, trade and military presence in Latin America, and its stated ambition to continue to broaden these ties. These new alliances are causing deep concern not only in the United States, but also in Europe and parts of Latin America. Others view the relations as an unthreatening and natural outgrowth of a rapidly changing, multi-polar world. There are points of agreement and divergence among different camps, as well as larger issues that must be addressed in order to come as close as possible to obtaining a full picture of what Iran's interests and intentions imply.

The Shared Understanding

There is broad agreement that Iran's expanding ties with Venezuela, forged by the personal friendship between Presidents Mahmoud Ahmadinejad and Hugo Chávez respectively, anchor the relationships in the region. Iran's relationships with Ecuador's Rafael Correa and Bolivia's Evo Morales clearly pass through Venezuela and are a direct result of the convergent interests of Iran and Venezuela in building these alliances. Iran's relationship with Nicaragua is slightly different, given President Daniel Ortega's long-standing personal relationship with the Iranian revolution, dating back to his first term as president (1979-1990). Nonetheless even Ortega's relationship with Iran is closely tied to his relationship with Chávez, because Nicaragua is far more dependent on Chávez's discounted oil than any of his other regional allies.

A second point of general agreement is that Iran, facing broad international sanctions because of its non-transparent nuclear program, is primarily seeking political support and leverage against the United States, rather than deep economic relationships in Latin America. The notable exceptions are ventures related to strategic minerals or hydrocarbons.

Related to this is the third point of convergence: Iran's overall dealings on the economic and diplomatic fronts are generally opaque, built on the personal dynamic between Ahmadinejad and Latin American heads of state, as demonstrated by the numerous personal visits conducted by and among Ahmadinejad, Chávez, Ortega, Morales and Correa. These personalized relationships have largely supplanted institutionalized, formal policies guided by input from the respective congresses or ministries of foreign affairs and economic issues. This is particularly clear in the cases of Ecuador (see Montúfar) and Nicaragua (see Maradiaga and Meléndez).

This stands in contrast to Iran's relationship with Brazil, where the ties are institutionalized and largely devoid of the personal diplomacy prevalent in the rest of the region. When institutional, rather than personal relationships, prevail, Iran overtures are often rejected or forced into more transparent plane.

An important result of such an institutionalized relationship is that Brazil refused to help Venezuela with is nuclear program after it became clear that Venezuela was not willing to proceed without the direct involvement of Iran. Ahmadinejad has been unable to visit Brazil, despite various efforts to do so.

While Iran's nuclear program is often portrayed as primarily a concern of the United States--and Iran's defiant rhetoric almost exclusively aimed at the Bush administration-- Iran has been sanctioned three times by the United Nations Security Council for its unwillingness to halt its uranium enrichment program.[1] This is important in viewing Iran's actions in Latin America and its attempts to expand its diplomatic reach and avoid international isolation.

Venezuela had sought a uranium enrichment technology transfer from Brazil in October 2005. The prospect of Iranian involvement led Brazilian officials to retract any initial enthusiasm for the deal. A spokesman for Brazil's Ministry of Science and Technology stated: "In view of possible Iranian participation, as President Chávez has suggested, such a partnership would be risky for Brazil," adding that, "Brazil is not interested in cooperating with countries that do not follow international treaties and whose programs are not monitored by competent authorities."[2] Argentina took a similar position, based on its long-standing tensions with Iran.[3] Venezuela did, finally, sign an agreement with Russia to build a nuclear power plant, in September 2008. While Iran's participation was not explicitly mentioned, Atomstroyexport, the same company building the Bushehr reactor in Iran, is expected to be the project operator in Venezuela.[4]

A final, and perhaps most important point of agreement is that a primary, and perhaps sole real point of convergence between Ahmadinejad and Chávez in forging their relationship is both of these leaders' openly declared hostility toward the United States and its allies in the region, and, to a lesser degree, the European Union and U.N. backers of the sanctions regime. As Brun noted, the meetings between Ahmadinejad and Chávez (as well as with Morales, Correa and Ortega) have become "occasions ...to attack the United States in the name of the struggle against imperialism and capitalism." As Farhi notes, these leaders relish the angst their relationship causes Washington. Ortega has declared the Iranian and Nicaraguan revolutions are "twin revolutions, with the same objectives of justice, liberty, sovereignty and peace...despite the aggressions of the imperialist policies." Ahmandinejad couched the alliances as part of "a large anti-imperialist movement that has emerged in the region."

Indeed, this common desire to build an alternative power structure free of the dominance of the United States is one of the few reasons that populist and self-described revolutionary, staunchly secular governments in Latin America (many who have been directly at odds with the Catholic church, the main religious force in their countries) would make common cause with a reactionary, theocratic Islamist regime.

Trade relations are still minimal, particularly when compared to commercial ties to the United States. There is little shared history or religious heritage, and virtually no cultural bonds. Only a shared platform of deep dislike for a common enemy--and the desire to recruit allies in the cause--can explain this otherwise improbable alliance. Iran's entry to Latin America has been possible, as Brun notes, as "an outgrowth of mounting criticism among Latin American governments of U.S. foreign policy." In addition to the strain of U.S. policy in Iraq has caused, there is the perceived lack of interest in the region by the Bush administration. The multiple visits of Ahmadinejad and senior Iranian officials to Latin

America and reciprocal state visits signal far more high-level interest in the region than the Bush administration is perceived to have.

The Crucial Dichotomy

This is a key question which must be addressed in any discussion of Iran's relationship to Latin America's populist governments. The above-noted yawning chasm between the Bolivarian Revolution's stated goals publicly embraced by Chávez, Ortega, Correa and Morales, and those of Ahmadinejad's revolutionary Islamist government. The Bolivarian revolution claims as principles equality, secularism, socialism, women's rights, and mass participation in governing. These are directly opposed to the goals of creating a theocracy where women's rights are denied, democratic participation is circumscribed by religious dictates and theologians set social and economic policy based on their interpretation of Koran, rather than the writing of Simón Bolívar. This lack of a more broad-based set of shared values helps explain Iran's behavior in the region. One explanation can be found by looking at Iran's promised economic aid, often undelivered, and its promises of diplomatic relations, which are promptly fulfilled.

Iran has signed billions of dollars in bilateral agreements with Venezuela, although financial accountability and monitoring is almost nonexistent.[5] Iran has also promised hundreds of millions of dollars in aid and investments in Nicaragua, Bolivia, and Ecuador. Because most of the deals are opaque and there are few public records available, it is not clear how much of the promised aid has been delivered. Maradiaga and Melédez clearly show the difficulties of discerning this in the case of Nicaragua, where Iran promised multiple projects, including $350 million deep-water canal and $120 million hydroelectric plant.[6] Yet they were unable to obtain information on the progress and expenditures on any of the major projects or loans.

Montúfar shows that Ecuador has made little effort to follow through on the verbal economic agreements between Correa and Ahmadinejad during Ahmadinejad's Jan. 15, 2007 visit to Quito when Correa was sworn in. There is little available information on the fate of the promised $1.1 billion in investment in Bolivia in the next five years.[7]

In contrast, the results of the promised diplomatic expansion are clearly visible. Post revolutionary Iran has had embassies in Cuba, Argentina, Uruguay, Brazil, Mexico and Venezuela.[8] In 2007, Iran reopened its embassies in Colombia[9] and in Nicaragua.[10] (Iran had closed its embassy in Nicaragua following the defeat of Ortega in the 1990 Presidential elections.)[11] Following a February 2007 meeting in Tehran Iranian Foreign Minister Manoucher Mottaki announced plans to reopen embassies in Chile, Ecuador and Uruguay, and launch a representative office in Bolivia, to be followed by a full embassy.[12] The ties are growing in both directions. In 2007, Ortega announced Nicaragua would open an embassy in Tehran while Morales announced that he is moving Bolivia's only embassy in the Middle East from Cairo to Tehran. [13]

The expanding diplomatic ties clearly give Iran a broader platform for pressing its international agenda, primarily the avoidance of international sanctions for its nuclear program and blunting efforts at international condemnation in the United Nations and other international forums. What is more difficult to calculate, but must be included in assessing Iran's goals, is Iran's history of using its embassies to support activities of the Quds Force (the special forces branch of the Iranian Revolutionary Guard Corps, formed as the main security force in Iran following the 1979 revolution) and Hezbollah (the Party of God) operatives.[14] Alconada Mon shows the Quds Force and Hezbollah, which often operate cooperatively, are jointly implicated in the AMIA case in Argentina, while also outlining the flawed police work and judicial handling in the case.

Another opaque aspect of Iran's activities in Latin America is the selective recruitment of government cadres and students by the Iranian government in the countries where they have strong ties. The classes, lasting from 30 to 90 days, are described as "diplomatic training," not something that Iran is particularly suited to teach to countries in the West. The classes, given in and around Tehran, include intelligence training, crowd control techniques, and counterintelligence. So far the training has involved several hundred people from Venezuela, Bolivia, Nicaragua, Ecuador and the Communist Party of El Salvador.[15] Given Iran's apparent lack of true "diplomatic" classes in these courses, one has to ask what the ultimate training is for, and whom it benefits.

Ties That Merit Further Examination

Because of the personalized nature and opaque relationships between Ahmadinejad and his Latin American allies there exists the potential, at least, for these alliances to be considered more than just an axis of annoyance. Venezuela is of particular concern because Chávez has taken several steps that point to a calculation that allowing Iran to evade the international sanctions regime is in his own interest. Such activity lies beyond the normal scope of relations between two nations with little in common except oil production and aspirations to form an anti-U.S. coalition.

Among the least explored elements is the Iranian financial presence in Venezuela and its possible use to help Iran avoid the international sanctions on its banking institutions. The primary Iranian banking vehicle is Venezuela Banco Internacional de Desarrollo (BID), established in September 2007. The Toseyeh Saderat Iran bank owns all the 40 million shares of the bank, and each share is valued at 1,000 bolivars, the currency of Venezuela. All seven of the bank directors, as well as their seven alternates, are Iranian citizens.[16] The Saderat bank group was designated by the U.S. Treasury Department's Office of Foreign Asset Controls (OFAC) in October 2007 as a financial vehicle for the government of Iran to fund Hezbollah, Hamas and other terrorist groups and helping Iran evade the international financial sanctions put in place by the international community.[17] As noted earlier, the Saderat group is also under U.N. sanction as well, as part of the effort to cut off Iran's access to international banking institutions to fund its nuclear program. The irregular circumstances surrounding the formation of the bank, the unusual speed with which its charter was approved and its entirely foreign leadership makes it worthy of further study.

A second financial vehicle is the Banco Binacional Iraní-Venezolano, established May 19, 2008, with an initial capitalization of $1.2 billion, half put in by each country. The stated purpose of the bank is to finance activities in the areas of industry, trade, infrastructure, housing, energy, capital markets and technology. The bank will also issue bonds to be placed on the international capital markets and execute cooperation and technical assistance agreements with third parties."[18] Yet I was unable to find any public record of any project being financed by these funds.

Another unusual feature of the Iran-Venezuela relationship is the March 2008 inauguration of direct flights between Caracas and Tehran, returning via Damascus, Syria. Either Boeing 747s or Airbus 340s, operated under a code share agreement between Venezuela's state-controlled Conviasa airlines and Iran's national carrier, Air Iran, carry out the weekly flights. This is unusual given the almost total absence of tourism and relative paucity of commercial ties between the two countries. Iran's ambassador in Venezuela said such large aircraft were necessary for the flight because Chávez is "much loved in our country, and our people want to come and get to know this land."[19] No known records of the passengers and cargo on the flights are maintained, and visas are not required.[20]

The concerns about these and unusual activities, cloaked in official secrecy, would be more easily dismissed if not for a longstanding and complex web of relationships between state and non-state actors that carry across Iran's relationships with its Latin American allies.

Iran is the primary sponsor of Hezbollah, a designated terrorist organization by the United States, and one that has carried out numerous attacks against American citizens, as well being a likely participant in the attacks a decade ago in Argentina. Iran, in turn, has a cordial relationship with Chávez, who, in turn has developed a deep relationship with the Revolutionary Armed Forces of Colombia (Fuerzas Armadas Revolucionarias de Colombia-FARC) in neighboring Colombia.[21] The FARC is also a designated terrorist organization by the United States[22] and the European Union.[23] In September 2008 the Treasury Department's OFAC sanctioned three of Chávez's closest associates, including two intelligence chiefs, for aiding the FARC in the purchase of weapons and drug trafficking.[24] The FARC has a long history of making alliances with other terrorist organizations across ideological and geographic boundaries, including the Provisional Irish Republican Army (P-IRA) and ETA separatists in Spain.[25] Another prominent regional player, Ortega in Nicaragua, has maintained a close relationship with both the FARC and Iran for more than two decades. The common denominators among the state protagonists are a strongly anti-U.S. platform and sponsorship of non-state armed groups operating outside their national borders. It is therefore necessary to ask whether the non-state actors, protected by their state sponsors, will themselves form alliances that will threaten the stability of the region, as well as that of the United States. Of primary concern is a possible Hezbollah-FARC alliance, centered on training of armed groups and drug trafficking.

There are public allegations of Chávez's direct support for Hezbollah, among them the June 18, 2008 OFAC designations of two Venezuelan citizens, including a senior diplomat, as terrorist supporters for working with the armed group. Several businesses were also sanctioned. Among the things the two are alleged to have been doing on behalf of Hezbollah were coordinating possible terrorist attacks and building Hezbollah-sponsored community centers in Venezuela.[26]

There is a long history of outside terrorist actors being active in Latin America, in addition to those in Argentina discussed by Alcona Mon. These include, in addition to ETA and the P-IRA in Colombia, the documented visits in the late 1990s to the Tri-Border Area of Hezbollah's chief of logistics Immad Mugnyiah (now deceased) and Khalid Sheikh Mohammed, the architect of the 9/11 attacks on New York and Washington and currently held in Guantanamo.[27] There is the possible presence of Osama bin Laden in the region in 1995, as reported by the Brazilian, French and U.S. media.[28] Given the security with which these senior operatives would have to move it is unlikely they would visit the region unless there were adequate security arrangements and infrastructure to allow them to operate. It is also unlikely they would travel there if there were no reason to do so.

Conclusions

Multiple factors, when taken together, point to Iran being more than a mere irritant in one of the most important and geographically proximate spheres of influence of the United States. Because the Iranian presence is based almost exclusively on a shared anti-U.S. agenda among the principal actors, and the ties of the Chávez and Ahmadinejad governments to armed non-state actors, Iran's presence is potentially destabilizing not only to the United States but to the region.

The Iranian presence is due in no small measure to the sharp turn toward populism, with a strong anti-U.S. component, in recent elections across Latin America. The ascendency of radical populism is due in part to the corruption and inability of the prior "neo-liberal" governments to seriously curtail poverty. This shift has allowed Iran, operating through Venezuela, to spread its influence largely by invitation, using the promise (often unfulfilled) of significant economic aid. There is one sign of the lack of public accountability and transparency in the economic dealings between Iran and Venezuela and its allies in Latin America.

The hemispheric picture is clouded by the close relationship of Chávez and Ortega to the FARC, an insurgency seeking to overthrow a democratically elected (although flawed, particularly in the field of human rights) government in neighboring Colombia and promoting armed revolution in other Latin American countries.[29] Given Iran's ties to Hezbollah and Venezuela, Venezuela's ties to Iran and the FARC, the FARC's history of building alliances with other armed groups, and the presence of Hezbollah and other armed Islamist groups in Latin America, it would be imprudent to dismiss this alignment as an annoyance.

Given the global recession, low oil prices, the necessity of Venezuela to maintain a U.S. market for its oil, and the deep economic ties between the United States and Latin America, the long-term extent of Iran ultimate threat remains unclear. The ability of Iran and Venezuela to present a viable anti-U.S. agenda and support non-state groups will likely be in direct proportion to the world price of oil.

Iran is spending scarce resources on courting Latin America, seizing the opportunity to break its international isolation while significantly improving its intelligence and logistical capabilities in an area of vital strategic value to the United States. Iran's presence is felt more acutely because of the absence of a U.S. agenda that is broadly embraced by Latin Americans, particularly since the 9/11 attacks. While the scope of the threat is open to debate, the intentions of Iran and is allies, led by Venezuela, should not be underestimated or dismissed.

Notes

1 Kay Farley, "U.N. Adds New Set of Iran Sanctions," *Los Angeles Times*, March 4, 2008, p. A06. The sanctions include a travel ban on senior Iranian officials, the freezing of assets of companies believed to be involved in the nuclear program, the right to inspect cargo in ports and airports, and the monitoring of

Bank Melli and Bank Saderat, believed to be financing the purchase of nuclear technologies.

2 Andrei Khalip, "Brazil Wary on Nuclear Cooperation with Venezuela," *Reuters*, May 23, 2005.

3 Mariela Leon and Marianna Parraga, "Negotiations to Purchase Nuclear Reactor from Argentina Confirmed," *El Universal*, October 11, 2005, http://www.eluniversal.com/2005/10/11/en_pol_art_11A618849.shtml, Media reports noted that discussion over selling Venezuela nuclear technology in Argentina had pitted the "pro-Chávez" camp against the "anti-Chávez" camp. See Natasha Niebieskikwiat, "Venezuela quiere comprarle un reactor nuclear a la Argentina, *Clarín*, October 9, 2005, http://www.clarin.com/diario/2005/10/09/elpais/p-00315.htm

4 *Russica-Izvestia Information*, September 30, 2008, and *Agence France-Presse*, "Venezuela Wants to Work With Russia on Nuclear Energy: Chávez," September 29, 2008.

5 The figures of the projects are difficult to determine and require further study. Since 2001 the two nations have signed some 180 trade agreements, with the total value, if the investment actually occurs, of $7 billion. See: *Moj News Agency*, "Iran-Venezuela Strengthen Economic-Ideological Ties, October 8, 2008; and Nasser Karimi, "Chavez, Ahmadinejad: US Power on Decline," The *Associated Press*, Tuesday, November 20, 2007, accessed at: http://www.washingtonpost.com/wp-dyn/content/article/2007/11/19/AR2007111900400.html

6 See Todd Bensman, "Iran Making Push Into Nicaragua," *San Antonio Express News*, December 18, 2007; and "Iran Offers Aid to Nicaragua, in a Sign of Deepening Ties," *Reuters* , August 6, 2007.

7 BBC Monitoring Middle East-Political, " Iran Wants to 'Exploit' Bolivian Uranium," September 22, 2008. This is the translated text of what appeared in the Iranian newspaper *Kargozaran* on September 2, 2008.

8 Statement by Kucinich, op cit.

9 "Colombia Seeking Energy Cooperation," Iran Daily, op cit.

10 Todd Bensman, "Iran making push into Nicaragua," *San Antonio Express News*, op cit.

11 "Irán abrirá embajada en Managua y Nicaragua en Teherán," *El Nuevo Diario*, op cit.

12 Remarks by Ambassador Jaime Daremblum, Hudson Institute, at the Conference on "Creating an Environment for Trans- America Security Cooperation," Florida International University, Miami, May 3-4, 2007.

13 *Associated Press*, "Bolivia Moving Mideast Embassy to Iran from Egypt, " September 5, 2008.

14 For a more complete look at the relationship between the IRGC, the Quds Force, international intelligence gathering and ties to Hezbollah and other designated terrorist groups, see: Anthony H. Cordesman, "Iran's Revolutionary Guards, the al Quds Force, and other Intelligence and Paramilitary Forces

(Working Draft)," Center for Strategic and International Studies, August 16, 2007. Cordesman notes that "The Quds are also believed to play a continuing role in training, arming, and funding Hezbollah in Lebanon and to have begun to support Shi'ite militia and Taliban activities in Afghanistan." (p. 8). He also notes that: "The Quds has offices or 'sections' in many Iranian embassies, which are closed to most embassy staff. It is not clear whether these are integrated with Iranian intelligence operations or if the ambassador in each embassy has control of, or detailed knowledge of, operations by the Quds staff. However, there are indications that most operations are coordinated between the IRGC and offices within the Iranian Foreign Ministry and MOIS." (page 9).

15 The information is derived from author interviews with people in Nicaragua (FSLN) and El Salvador (FMLN-PC) who separately attended different types of training in Tehran, and described, separately, different types of training given. The FMLN-PC is the sector of the FMLN that maintains close ties to Chávez and Iran, while other sectors of the FMLN are opposed to such close ties.

16 Founding BID documents in possession of the author. The Treasury Department's Financial Crimes Enforcement Network (FinCEN) issued a warning against several Iranian banks, including BID, viewable at: http://www.fincen.gov/statutes_regs/guidance/pdf/fin-2008-a002.pdf;

17 http://www.ustreas.gov/press/releases/hp644.htm.

An OFAC designation allows the U.S. government to seize any U.S.-based assets of the designated entity, as well as making it illegal for that entity to do any business in the United States, or for any U.S. company or person to do business with the designated entity. The list is widely used by international financial institutions as part of their "know your customer" due diligence research.

18 "Iranian-Venezuelan Bank Organized by Law," *El Universal*, May 21, 2008, accessed at: http://english.eluniversal.com/2008/05/21/imp_en_eco_art_iranian-venezuelan-b_21A1594761.shtml

19 Simon Romero, "Venezuela and Iran Strengthen Ties With Caracas-to-Tehran Flight," *New York Times*, March 3, 2007.

20 United States Department of State, Country Reports on Terrorism, March 2008, Chapter 2.

21 The most compelling primary source evidence of this relationship comes from the computer of Raúl Reyes, the FARC's deputy commander killed March 1, 2008 when Colombian troops raided his command center in neighboring Ecuador. Colombian troops recovered some 600 gigabytes of information from several computers and memory sticks found in the camp. Interpol, after conducting an independent analysis, concluded the data had not been tampered with when For a more complete analysis of what the documents show, see: Douglas Farah, "What the FARC Papers Show Us About Latin American Terrorism," The NEFA Foundation, April 1, 2008, accessible at: http://www.nefafoundation.org/miscellaneous/FeaturedDocs/nefafarc0408.pdf

22 "FARC Terrorist Indicted for 2003 Grenade Attack on Americans in Colombia," Department of

Justice Press Release, September 7, 2004. accessed at:

http://www.usdoj.gov/opa/pr/2004/September/04_crm_599.htm.

23 Official Journal of the European Union, Council Decision of Dec. 21, 2005, accessed at: http://europa.eu.int/eurlex/

24 The three are Hugo Armando Cavajál, director of military intelligence, described as providing weapons to the FARC; Henry de Jesus Rangél, director of the civilian Directorate of Intelligence and Prevention Services, described as protecting FARC drug shipments; and Ramón Emilio Rodriguez Chacín, who, until a few days before the designation was Venezuela's minster of interior and justice. He is described as the "Venezuelan government's main weapons contact for the FARC." The role of the three in closely collaborating with the FARC is described in some detail in the documents captured in the Reyes documents. See: "Treasury Targets Venezuelan Government Officials Supporting the FARC," Press Room, Department of Treasury, September 12, 2008, viewed at: http://www.treas.gov/press/releases/hp1132.htm.

25 For a more detailed look at the relationship between the FARC and other terrorist organizations, see: Douglas Farah, "The FARC's International Relations: A Network of Deception," The NEFA Foundation, September 22, 2008, accessed at: http://www.nefafoundation.org/miscellaneous/FeaturedDocs/nefafarcirnetworkdeception0908.pdf

26 One of those designated, Ghazi Nasr al Din, who served as the charge d'affaires of Venezuelan embassy in Damascus, and then served in the Venezuelan embassy in London. The OFAC statement said that in late January 2006, al Din facilitated the travel of two Hezbollah representatives of the Lebanese parliament to solicit donation and announce the opening of a Hezbollah-sponsored community center and office in Venezuela. The second individual, Fawzi Kan'an is described as a Venezuela-based Hezbollah supporter and a "significant provider of financial support to Hizbollah." He met with senior Hezbollah officials in Lebanon to discuss operational issues, including possible kidnapping and terrorist attacks. The OFAC statement can be accessed at: http://www.treas.gov/press/releases/hp1036.htm

27 For a comprehensive look at possible radical Islamist activities in the region, see: Rex Hudson, "Terrorist and Organized Crime Groups in the Tri-Border (TBA) of South America," Federal Research Division, Library of Congress, July 2003. For more recent Hezbollah ties, as related by Colombia authorities, see: "Colombia Ties Drug Ring to Hezbollah," *Reuters* News Agency, as appeared in the *New York Times*, Oct. 22, 2008.

28 "El Esteve no Brazil," *Veja* on-line, no. 1,794, March 19, 2003; "Bin Laden Reportedly Spent Time in Brazil in '95," *Washington Post*, March 18, 2003, p. A24.

29 Farah, "The FARC's International Relations: A Network of Deception," op cit.

TEHRAN'S PERSPECTIVE ON IRAN-LATIN AMERICAN RELATIONS

Farideh Farhi

The proper context of the current relationship between Iran and Latin America is probably best captured in a statement made by Ali-Reza Sheikh Attar, Iran's deputy foreign minister, in a news conference in January 2008 during his two-day stay in Mexico City. According to Sheikh-Attar, "given far distance between Iran and Latin America, the Latin American countries did not enjoy a proper position in Iran's foreign policy in the past, but the Ninth Government[1] gives priority to promotion of ties with these countries."[2]

I begin with this seemingly insignificant statement because of the basic accuracy of it: that the attention that Iran is giving Latin America as a collectivity or region is something relatively new, dating back to the election of a new president in 2005. Furthermore, this recent attention is acknowledged as new by members of Iran's current administration and is represented as part and parcel of a new "aggressive foreign policy" that is touted by Mahmoud Ahmadinejad as needed, instead of the previous administration's "passive" foreign policy, to counter policies by other countries, specifically the United States, to isolate Iran. As such, it must be understood more as a policy or political orientation of the new government rather than a strategic reorientation of Iran's foreign policy.

By suggesting a new policy orientation that emphasizes the importance of Latin America as a region, the intent is not to ignore a history of Iran's relationship with particular Latin American countries. In fact, relations with individual countries in Latin America are nothing new. The Islamic Republic of Iran's relationship with Cuba has been a long standing one, mostly based on political and ideological kinship especially after the end of the Iran-Iraq War when Castro no longer had to calibrate his relationship with Iran in the light of his close relationship to Saddam Hussein.[3]

Iran and Venezuela have also had a long standing political relationship as co-founders of OPEC. This relationship, although not severed, was turned very tenuous after the Iranian revolution of 1979, to turn again into an alliance at OPEC and elsewhere with the rise of Hugo Chavez to power in 1998. As "price maximalists," as recently as June 2008, both Tehran and Caracas voiced their opposition to what they called Saudi Arabia's unilateral decision to increase crude oil production. And in the November 2007 OPEC in Riyadh, Saudi Arabia, both Iran and Venezuela (along with the recently re-joined member Ecuador) insisted on including in the summit's closing statement, successfully resisted by Saudi Arabia, concerns over the falling value of dollar.[4]

Beyond political and ideological links, attempts at improving trade and economic relations with individual Latin American countries are also not something invented by Iran's new administration. Thirteen Iran-Cuba scientific, technological and economic joint commissions have already been held and according to Iranian press reports Cuba-Iran trade now stands at 213 million Euros ($327.3 million) which is much higher than earlier reports of around $50 million in 2003.[5] Venezuela's Hugo Chavez first visited Tehran in 2001 and then in 2003 and it was during the former President Mohammad Khatami's February 2004 visit to Caracas to attend the summit of non-aligned G-15 that the setting up of a plant with a capacity to produce 5,000 tractors in Ciudad Bolivar was finalized (with Iran having a 31% stake in the Veniran tractor plant), ultimately opening the way for the assembly production of two Iranian designed cars (the so-called "first anti-imperialist cars") that recently began to be produced in Venezuela.[6] Venirauto sold its first batch of Samand sedan (called Centauro in Venezuela) in July 2007. It is jointly owned Iran Khodro, one of Iran's state-owned car company, and VENINSA, a Venezuelan industry investment company. Its plant's capacity is 26,000 cars per year. But it not clear how many is produced at this time but there are also plans to produce a second cheaper car, called Turpial in Venezuela, in cooperation with Iran's second biggest carmaker, SAIPA. This year, the company hopes to assemble about 8,000 cars. The plant will also produce tractors and other farm equipment.

And Venezuela and Cuba have not been the only countries of economic interest to Iran. On the side of the same G-15 summit meeting, Khatami met with the newly elected president Lula da Silva of Brazil and talked about bilateral trade with consequential results. Since then Brazil exports to Iran have doubled and Brazil in fact has been Iran's largest Latin American trade partner for several years, with its exports to Iran as high as those of neighboring Turkey and India.[7]

It is true that during the same G-15 summit meeting, if the Iranian papers are to be believed, despite Argentine president Nestor Kirshner's interest in discussing bilateral economic ties, Khatami refused to meet with him until "Buenos Aires formally apologizes to Tehran for falsely charging Iranian diplomats with involvement in the bombing of the AMIA Jewish community center in 1994."[8] But the fact is that Islamic Iran and Argentina used to have a relatively robust trade relationship mostly centered on the latter's beef and agricultural exports to Iran. And if the initial Argentinean version of the AMIA charges against Iran is to be believed, it was Iran's anger at the sudden reneging on the part of Argentina to deliver on its promise to sell nuclear technology and material that led to the bombing of the Argentine-Jewish Mutual Association.[9]

None of these bilateral relationships should come as a surprise. First, the essential non-alignment foundation of Iran's foreign policy creates the impetus for seeking economic and political relationship with countries Iran sees as committed, at least in principle, the idea of improved south-south relations. The shift to the left in many important Latin American countries in the latter part of 1990s but particularly in the first decade of the new millennium has allowed Iran to be a bit more successful in its attempt to improve relations with particular countries.

Secondly, the concerted and determined effort on the part of the United States since 1995 to isolate Iran politically and economically has also created the motivation for a more active foreign policy in order to prove wrong the asserted claim about Iran's international isolation. Finally, the election of a reformist president in Iran in 1997 made it possible for countries like Brazil to engage Iran with enough confidence to withstand pressures from the United States. It is true that the Iranian understanding of non-alignment has always been more ideological, rejectionist, moralistic, rigid, and quarrelsome than most other significant non-aligned movement (NAM) players such as India or Brazil but the election of Mohammad Khatami allowed other NAM movement players to count on Iran moving in a different direction.

Still it is important to note that throughout these initial years of improved bilateral relations between Iran and various Latin American countries, the two main orbits of Iran's foreign policy remained the Persian Gulf and Central Asia-Caucasus. Furthermore, during both the Hashemi Rafsanjani and Khatami presidencies, entailing the 16 year span of 1989 to 2005, the regional interest in Latin America was simply not there. As mentioned, Iran welcomed improved relations with particular countries but for combating its isolation on a regional basis, Iran looked more towards Africa than Latin America. Both of these presidents took multi-country tips to the African continent, setting the stage for the creation of the High Council for African Policy, which during Khatami's presidency was headed by his vice-president Mohammad-Reza Aref, with a special emphasis on economic and trade relationships.

Since 2005, however, Africa has received less attention Although Ahmadinejad has taken two trips to attend African Union and Organization of the Islamic Conference summits in Gambia and Senegal on his way to Latin America, he has yet to visit Africa as a guest of a country. On the other hand, his much touted and well publicized trips to Venezuela in July 2006, Venezuela, Nicaragua, and Ecuador in January 2007, and Venezuela and Bolivia[10] in September 2007, and his hosting of Chavez and Daniel Ortega in Iran[11] is a policy re-direction that entails a regional outlook - made possible by changes in Latin America and opportunistically capitalized upon by Ahmadinejad. The rising number of leftist leaders in Latin America and their growing frustration with or moving away from Washington has given Ahmadinejad an opportunity to exhibit his "aggressive foreign policy" which has been formulated as a rejection of what he considers to be Khatami's conciliatory, passive, and ultimately ineffective foreign policy to make points both internationally as well as to his domestic audience. From Ahmadinejad's point of view, rather than responding passively towards the US attempt to isolate Iran politically and economically and become the dominant player in the Middle East region, Iran's backyard, Iran should move aggressively in the United States' own backyard as a means to rattle it or at least make a point.

When analyzed closely, Ahmadinejad's regional approach to Latin American has three prongs:

- **Continuation and expansion of the bilateral strategy with was pursued by Khatami.** This strategy has essentially entailed quiet improvement of relationships involving visits by foreign and economic ministry officials and setting up of joint economic commissions (with Mexico and Brazil) and discussion of possible reopening of embassies in countries such as Chile.[12] In this context, the quiet nature of improvement, for instance with Brazil, has been more a reflection of exigencies imposed on Ahmadinejad than his own preference. For instance, Ahmadinejad had intended to disembark in Brasilia in September 2007 on an official visit, after speaking at the UN General Assembly and visiting Venezuela and Bolivia and Brazilian diplomacy came out with the classic excuse: the impossibility of reconciling Lula and the Iranian president's schedules, no doubt out of the concern that such a visit might bring increased pressure on Brazil to cut off its increasingly lucrative trade with Iran which is essentially a one way trade.[13] Still the hesitance to meet with Ahmadinejad did not prevent President Lula da Silva to publicly give support to Iran's nuclear energy program and suggest that Iran "should not be punished just because of Western suspicions it wants to make an atomic bomb."[14]

- **A highly publicized touting of the relationship with Venezuela and the creation of the so-called "axis of unity."** This relationship is not only relished by both leaders in economic and political terms, with Venezuela giving support to Iran's nuclear program, it is publicly touted by both as a poke in the eye of the United States. Farsnews, a wire service close to Ahmadinejad's government said it best in its lead sentence about Ahmadinejad's visit to Venezuela, identifying the visit as designed "to produce three things: tractors, influence and angst." The influence is presumably for Chavez and Ahmadinejad, two presidents who hope to project their prestige and power. The angst is of course for Washington. Chavez has even stated publicly said that the relationship annoys Washington and both men have joked about their "nuclear" relationship.[15]

- **Again a highly publicized relationship with the new governments of smaller countries of Bolivia, Nicaragua, and Ecuador**. To two of these countries, Iran has made economic promises in the form of investment in infrastructural development. In the case of Nicaragua this has meant a $350 million pledge along with Venezuela to build a deepwater seaport near Monkey Point on Nicaragua's Atlantic shore, then to plow a connecting "dry canal" corridor of pipelines, rails and highways across the country. Iran has also already set up am embassy in Managua. In Ecuador, Iran has opened a trade office in Quito in January 2008. While these relationships should be considered as part and parcel of Ahmadinejad's aggressive outlook towards foreign policy, engaging in outreach with anyone offering a welcome mat, for both external and internal purposes (especially relished because its aggressiveness is reflected in activities in US' back yard), it is really difficult to imagine that they will turn into anything significant, if at all.

The proposed building of Monkey Point seaport is facing resistance form local land right activists who have already resisted two attempted development efforts in the past decade. Considering that the proposed Nicaraguan projects are essentially sold to the Iranian populace as an aid to Nicaragua, signs of resistance on the part of the local population will either be seen as ingratitude or too much trouble for a policy based on political or symbolic value and not economic purposes.[16] The Iranian parliament, which has to approve funds for such projects, has yet to debate the issue. Iran's refusal to forgive Nicaragua's $152 million debt to Iran, despite, Ortega's explicit public request, should probably seen as the extent to which Iran's symbolic foreign policy is limited by economic considerations.[17]

Relationships with Ecuador and Bolivia are also likely to be kept in distance for now. Ecuador's new President Rafael Correa would benefit little from closer ties with Iran and, with half of his country threatening session, Morales probably has little time to entertain broader relations with Iran. In general it should be argued that the relationship Iran has developed with these countries is a subsidiary of its relationship with Venezuela and as such it is Venezuela that is in the driver seat in guiding these relationships not Iran.

To conclude Ahmadinejad's Latin policy can be summarized as follows:

- Iran's much touted recent interest in Latin America as a region has been very much a function of changing circumstances in Latin America.

- It is driven at this point by Venezuela and Iran's shared opposition to the United States and a desire to make Washington as nervous as possible about as many issues as possible and a shared desire to project their governments, both inside and outside of their respective countries, as fighting broadly for justice or a more just world order.

- By courting Venezuela and other Latin American leaders close to Chavez, it is political support rather than economic deals that Iran seeks. Given its political circumstances, Iran is working hard to push back Washington's effort to tarnish Iran's international reputation. Accordingly, Iran will take every opportunity to show that it is not isolated and in the process question Washington's influence even its own backyard.

- Ultimately, however, this is not a sustainable strategy for Iran in terms of its own domestic politics as well as long-term strategic calculations because Iran is not in the driver seat; Latin American circumstances and particular political calculations of individual Latin American countries are.

- The better and more likely bet for Iran, once Ahmadinejad is gone and he will be gone - if not in a year, in five years - is the same gradual improvement of bilateral relationships based on economic give and take and a modicum of shared commitment to principles of non-alignment.

Notes

1 Numbering the four year tenure of each president has become a tradition in post-revolutionary Iran. The "Ninth Government" refers to the current term of Mahmoud Ahmadinejad's presidency.

2 IRNA, 20 January 2008.

3 Fidel Castro visited Tehran in May 2001, receiving an honorary degree from Tarbiat Modares University and meeting with Iran's supreme leader, Ali Khamenei.

4 Nasser Karimi, "Chavez, Ahmadinejad: US Power in Decline." The Associated Press, 20 November 2007. http://www.washingtonpost.com/wp-dyn/content/article/2007/11/19/AR2007111900400_pf.html. During the OPEC meeting, Iran and Venezuela proposed that the cartel begin setting its oil prices based on a basket of currencies, rather than just the dollar, and they wanted the summit to specifically express concern over the dollar's slide in its final statement. Saudi Arabia blocked the move, "with its foreign minister cautioning that even talking publicly about the currency's decline could further hurt its value."

5 *Fars News Agency*, 20 June 2008. http://english.farsnews.com/newstext.php?nn=8703310656.

6 http://www.venirauto.com/home.

7 Brazil's exports to Iran focus on corn, soy and sugar but its interest in Iran is potentially beyond trade. In 2004, Petrobras (Brazilian Petroleum Corporation), injected $35 million in a joint project with Repsol of Spain. This initiative sparked serious criticism from the United States. This company is also interested in focusing on the exploration of Iranian blocs in the Caspian Sea. However, for now, it is limited by divestment campaigns in various states in the United States and threats of sanctions against companies doing business with Iran. . See, for instance, "State's Pensions, Brazil's Oil and Iran Entangled." *St. Petersburg Times*, 10 December 2007 (http://www.sptimes.com/2007/12/10/State/State_pensions__Brazi.shtml).

8 Tehran Times, 28 February 2004.

9 The AMIA case has gone through many ups and downs, involving prosecutorial changes, witness tampering charges as well as several arrests that ended in release. In 2007 Argentina was able to convince Interpol to issue Red Notices which are international wanted person notices for 5 Iranians and one Lebanese, including former Iranian officials. Iran immediately contested these notices for being "politically motivated" and based on "unfounded and undocumented charges." At this point, the dispute between the two member countries is going through Interpol's process of dispute resolution in which both parties have agreed to participate. See Ronal K. Noble, "Interpol Follows the Rules." *The Washington Times*, 24 January 2007.

10 During this visit Bolivia and Iran established relations for the first time. Iran and Bolivia also signed a number of bilateral agreements, including 100 mi-

llion dollars in Iranian financing for projects in Bolivia. See "Ahmadinejad Shores Up Support in Bolivia, Venezuela." AFP, 27 September 2007. http://afp.google.com/article/ALeqM5gkga-ABVZuKPBO0_8-qep6iWGANQ. None of this financing is yet to materialize.

11 Since Ahmadinejad's presidency, Chavez has visited Iran four times. Ortega had visited Iran once and was expected to visit again in June 2008 but this trip has yet to materialize. In November 2007 trip to Tehran, Chavez and Ahmadinejad signed four memorandums of understanding to create a joint bank, a fund, an oil industry technical training program and an industrial agreement. On Chavez's visit in July 2007, the two leaders broke ground for a joint petrochemical complex in Iran, with 51 percent in Iranian ownership and 49 percent owned by Venezuela. The two nations also began construction of a petrochemical complex in Venezuela, at a total combined cost of $1.4 billion. According to official reports, since 2001, the two countries have signed more than 180 trade agreements, worth more than $20 billion in potential investment, but the extent of actual implementation is not yet clear and it is doubtful that the amount of actual investment is even remotely close.

12 Iran currently has embassies in Argentina, Brazil, Colombia, Cuba, Mexico, Nicaragua, Uruguay, and Venezuela.

13 Denise Chrispim Marin: "Itamaraty Avoids Ahmadinejad, Lula Summit." *Agencia Estado* 25 September 2007.

14 "Brazil's Lula Defends Iran's Nuclear Rights." Reuters, 25 September 2007. http://www.reuters.com/article/topNews/idUSN2536221720070925, During a joint press conference with President Bush at Camp David Lula publicly defended Iran as "an important trade partner" with whom Brazil has "no political divergence." Rejecting US calls to shun the Iranian regime, Lula insisted, "we will continue to work together on what is in our national interest".

15 According to Chavez, "The two countries' cooperation has turned into a great unity between the Iranian and Venezuelan nations and this annoys the US imperialism." Fars News Agency, 24 April 2008.

16 In fact, there has already been public criticism of the Nicaraguan policy in Iran by both former reformist diplomats as well as in some conservative websites. For a criticism of Ahmadinejad's Nicaragua policy see an opinion piece by former deputy foreign minister Mohsen Aminzadeh called "after 25 Years." In this piece Aminzadeh recalls his first trip to Nicaragua in the early revolutionary days for symbolic and solidarity purposes and says while symbolism still should have a place in diplomacy, it cannot be the only aspect of diplomacy. http://www.irdiplomacy.ir/index.php?Lang=fa&Page=24&TypeId=5&ArticleId=211&Action=ArticleBodyView.

17 The forgiving of the debt is also not something that can be done by the president alone and must be approved by the Iranian parliament which has so far not been interested in doing so.

IRAN'S PLACE IN VENEZUELAN FOREIGN POLICY

ELODIE BRUN

The relationship between Iran and Venezuela is not just a function of the duo formed by Hugo Chávez and Mahmoud Ahmadinejad. Indeed, diplomatic ties between the two countries date back to 1947. The Shah also went to Venezuela for a state visit in 1975, and Carlos Andrés Pérez returned the favor two years later with a visit during a tour through the Middle East. Bilateral contacts have been maintained primarily in the context of cooperation on oil-related matters after the establishment of the Organization of Petroleum Exporting Countries (OPEC) in 1960, proposed at the time by Venezuela's Minister of Mines and Hydrocarbons.[1] Relations between Iran and Venezuela were maintained thereafter but at a low level of priority and in an international context that was vastly different from today, since the two countries were allied with the United States during the Cold War (until 1979 for Iran, when the Islamic Republic was created). Hugo Chávez's ascent to power energized the relationship beginning in 2000, when he took the first of several trips to the Middle East, including Iran, which was ruled at the time by Mohammad Khatami, who in turn made two visits to Venezuela.[2]

Given that it was Venezuela's president who pushed to resume ties with Iran, we may rightly ask how the diplomatic efforts that have been made toward bringing Venezuela and Iran closer together fit into Chávez's foreign policy. And is this strategy compatible with the international objectives Venezuela under Chávez has established since 1998?

The challenge is not to determine whether this policy is good or bad for Venezuela's future, but rather to analyze what it means in view of the international role Chávez is seeking to establish for Venezuela.

At the outset, Iran's international position and approach seem to mesh well with Chávez's foreign policy, especially since Ahmadinejad's rise to power. At the same time, Iran's stance also reveals the potential and the limits of the South-South policies the Venezuelan government is trying to promote in its global message.

Iran in Line with Hugo Chávez's Foreign Policy Objectives

Chávez's diplomatic approach to Iran complements Venezuela's own foreign policy objectives on issues the country has championed internationally since 1998, and on new topics that have arisen since Ahmadinejad became president of Iran in 2005.

Iran: Model of Key Points on Hugo Chávez's International Agenda

Iran and Venezuela are the second and fourth largest oil-producing countries, respectively, within OPEC, and although Venezuela originated the idea for the organization, the country was never a very active member. Chávez has opted for a much more assertive policy, however, aimed at using petroleum as a political tool.[3] As a result, he has defended high oil prices and was active in organizing the second summit of OPEC heads of state in Caracas in 2000. And in January 2007, Iran and Venezuela drafted a joint declaration confirming their desire to keep petroleum prices high and reiterating their wish to pursue a political agenda for OPEC at the November 2007 meeting at Riyadh.[4]

In addition to the challenges for oil-producing countries that it shares with Iran, Venezuela has embraced rhetoric on South-South solidarity. Venezuela's president often expresses his desire to diversify foreign relations, while also encouraging other developing countries to follow suit so as to reduce dependence on the twin superpowers, the United States and to a lesser extent, the European Union. His reaching out to a state that was isolated internationally by the major powers, like Iran, is consistent with this line of thinking. This policy also serves to underscore Venezuela's autonomy and independence, which are particularly important for Chávez. Furthermore, Iran and Venezuela are trying to team up to help other developing regions curb the influence from developed countries. For example, the two states signed an agreement with a

Malaysian private company in late 2007 aimed at creating a refinery in Syria to bolster the country's struggling production.[5] And Venezuelan Foreign Affairs Minister Nicolas Maduro said at the inauguration of the Fifth Joint Commission between Iran and Venezuela: "This alliance will give us little ones the right to exist."[6]

In view of the Venezuelan president's vow to aid other developing countries in diversifying their global ties, his attempt to introduce Iran to his Latin American neighbors is a logical first step. This desire for regional support is even inscribed in the official document *Líneas Generales del Plan de Desarrollo Económico y Social de la Nación 2001-2007* (General Guidelines for the Nation's Economic and Social Development 2001-2007).[7] In fact, some of the contacts created between Latin American states and Ahmadinejad's Iran have resulted in visits by the Iranian leader to South America. Obviously, the countries that feel the strongest connections to Iran are those closest to Chávez's government on a regional level. Accordingly, during his tour in January and visit in September 2007, Ahmadinejad met with the presidents of Bolivia, Ecuador, and Nicaragua. Iran has also officially expressed its desire to become a member of the Bolivarian Alternative for the People of Latin America and the Caribbean (ALBA),[8] which was launched with Venezuela's backing to promote an alternative regional integration strategy to the United States' Free Trade Area of the Americas (FTAA).[9] An international fair was to be held by ALBA in Teheran from 10-13 July 2008 to strengthen these connections.[10] Forging these ties is one way for Iran to end its international isolation while enhancing Chávez's regional role as Iran's gatekeeper. Dan Erikson has even described the Venezuelan president as a "manager" and godfather of the relationship between Iran and its Latin American allies.[11] This initial warming to the Islamic regime is also an outgrowth of the mounting criticism among Latin American governments of US foreign policy, providing an easy opportunity for Iran to make connections in Latin America. During his first trip in early 2007, the Iranian president proposed, among other things, the creation of an anti-American alliance, declaring: "Fortunately, a large anti-imperialist movement has emerged in this region."[12] However, not all the Latin American countries hold this attitude, the notable exceptions being Brazil and Argentina.[13] Iran is indeed a significant trade partner of Brazil,[14] but in adhering to a certain pragmatism and a desire to keep good relations with all its international partners, Brazil has maintained some distance from Iran, and Ahmadinejad has not visited there during his Latin American tours.[15] Argentina's case is special because it has kept its distance from Iran since 1994; in fact, Nestor Kirschner canceled his appearance at Rafael Correa's inauguration when he learned the Iranian leader would be present, rather than out of hostility toward the man.[16]

A close relationship with Iran thus harmonizes well with Venezuela's foreign policy objectives, especially since Ahmadinejad was elected president in 2005.

Good Timing: Overlapping Tenures, More Issues in Common since 2005

During his trip to Teheran in November 2004 to inaugurate a statue of Simón Bolívar, Chávez met the city's mayor at the time, Mahmoud Ahmadinejad, who welcomed him with the declaration: "Iran and the nations of Latin America are fighting for liberty and encouraging anti-colonialist revolts in other countries."[17] The fact that their tenures in office have overlapped since 2005 has led to a deepening of the relationship, including a significant increase in their bilateral meetings: Chávez has since visited Iran three times, on 29–30 July 2006, 1–2 July 2007, and 19 November 2007, and for his part, Ahmadinejad visited Venezuela on 17 September 2006, 13 January 2007, and 27 September 2007.

The most obvious link between the two presidents' foreign policies is their openly declared hostility toward the United States. In *Jugando con el globo. La política exterior de Hugo Chávez*, political scientist Carlos Romero wrote that "Anti-Americanism has become a spearhead in Venezuelan diplomacy."[18] Consequently, turning toward Iran, which has had no diplomatic relations with the US since the hostage crisis in 1979,[19] suits the logic of Chávez's foreign policy, especially considering that Iran's president adopts the same posture of condemnation, in particular in relation to George W. Bush's administration.[20] Thus their meetings have become occasions for the two leaders to attack the United States in the name of the struggle against imperialism and capitalism. During his visit to Iran in July 2007, Chávez declared: "Cooperation among independent countries, in particular between Iran and Venezuela, will be an important factor in the defeat of imperialism and in the victory of the people."[21]

Moreover, the two presidents both have a strategy of using global forums to voice their views, and they share a talent for oratory and a radical viewpoint. French analyst Thérèse Delpech notes that Ahmadinejad's thunderous style recalls that of his Venezuelan counterpart.[22] Other analysts emphasize the rhetorical flourish and power of their words, concluding that "they like making the big headlines."[23] It is clear that this strategy is what provides the greatest visibility to their bilateral relationship on the world scene, giving their demands a wider audience. They take advantage of their petrodollars to assert their presence on the global stage, which they themselves qualify as revolutionary. Chávez welcomed the Iranian president in September 2006 with the following words: "Two revolutions are now joining hands: the Persian people, warriors of the Middle East [...], and the sons of Simón Bolívar, warriors of the Caribbean, free peoples."[24]

The oratory style adopted by Venezuela and Iran is linked to their international agenda, which is actually more of a counter-agenda, since it advocates opposition to the neo-liberal model and promotes a multipolar world, a theme that is much more widespread today than at the time Venezuela began asserting it, for example in the *Líneas Generales del Plan de Desarrollo Económico y Social de la Nación 2001-2007.*[25] Chávez thus rows against the diplomatic currents, and his establishment of ties with Iran is a symbol of this.[26] One example of his intention to break with the established order is in the information sector: Iran and Venezuela want to challenge the supremacy of North American international broadcasting channels. Toward this end, Venezuela created *Telesur* in 2005 along with Argentina, Cuba, and Uruguay, and two years later, Iran announced the launching of *Press TV.*[27]

To reiterate, Iran fits well into Chávez's foreign policy objectives, which the Islamic country both symbolizes and shares, especially since 2005. Nonetheless, the strength of this relationship will also depend on the material outcome of their proposals.

A Bilateral Relationship Trying to Find Its Way

The Iran-Venezuela relationship is often analyzed in terms of its four pillars: political, military, economic, and cultural.

On the political front, besides the increase in bilateral meetings, Venezuela has supported Iran in its test of strength with the international community over suspicions about its program of uranium enrichment. When Ahmadinejad visited Caracas in September 2006, Chávez declared: "We support Iran's right to develop atomic energy for peaceful purposes."[28] In fact, Venezuela came through on its promise of support, and it was the only country to oppose the International Atomic Energy Agency's (IAEA) resolution GOC/2005/77 of September 2005 accusing Iran of violating its obligations under the 1978 Treaty on the Non-Proliferation of Nuclear Weapons. Venezuela also reiterated its opposition, followed by Cuba and Syria, to resolution GOV/2006/14 of 4 February 2006 aimed at transferring the case to the United Nations' Security Council.[29] The debate about possible ties between the Lebanon-based Hezbollah and Iran has also moved to Latin American territory. In fact, some fear that Hezbollah may have settled in Venezuela in the wake of its new ties to the Islamic Republic. Several reports have been published, primarily from the United States, about the presence of Hezbollah in the "Tri-Border Region" between Argentina, Brazil, and Paraguay, although no documents make concrete mention yet of what still remains hearsay.

In spite of the fact that the media often makes allusions to suspected military exchanges between Iran and Venezuela, it remains uncertain whether they are in fact taking place. Some declarations have been made, but to date there has been no official follow-up.[30] In this regard, Venezuela's relations with Russia appear to be more relevant.

There is much debate on the economic nature of the bilateral relationship between Iran and Venezuela. One of Chávez's objectives is to make use of his country's petroleum revenues to diversify Venezuela's economy, but to do so, he needs cooperation, and accordingly, he has turned to Iran, hoping to take advantage of its greater technological capacity.[31] The two presidents have signed numerous economic agreements in a variety of different sectors. In April 2008, during the two countries' Fifth Joint Commission held in Caracas, 192 projects were listed, of which 16 were under negotiation.[32] In the majority of cases, however, a given project requires the signing of several contracts marking the different stages of its implementation, meaning that there are more signed documents than there are projects. The economic agreements involve sectors ranging from the construction of factories for tractors, automobiles, bicycles, milk treatment, and corn processing to scientific and medical cooperation, also including participation by Iranian technicians in transportation and the construction of housing.[33] According to some analysts, such as Carlos Malmund and Carlota García Encina of the Real Instituto Elcano in Spain, there has been no follow-up on most of the agreements or the promises of investments. They recognize, however, that economic issues play an essential role in Iran-Venezuela relations.[34] According to figures available from the COMTRADE database at the World Trade Organization, trade between Iran and Venezuela has fluctuated over time, but during the last three years it increased dramatically, notably because there had been so little to begin with. In 1998, trade between the two countries totaled $5.8 million but fell to $188,626 in 2001. Since then, trade increased to $1.1 million in 2004, $14.5 million in 2005, and it reached $50.7 million in 2006, the highest level in their bilateral trade history.[35] In fact, the two countries have committed to trade amounting to nearly $20 billion, but most of their agreements are works in progress, and only time will tell if this trend will be sustained. From this perspective, how trade between the two nations evolves in the coming years will reveal something about the two countries' ability to ensure their demands are met. In 2006, Venezuela imported $37.4 million worth of Iranian goods, and Iran imported $13.3 million of Venezuelan goods. On the balance sheet, Venezuela has a trade deficit with Iran, but this reflects the nature of their cooperation agreements on projects, the majority of which take place on Venezuelan territory. The flow of goods also highlights those sectors of the economy that benefit most from their relationship: in 2006, Venezuela's main imports from Iran were chemical, pharmaceutical, and medical products, machinery, and transportation and farming equipment including tractors; conversely, Iran imports from Venezuela included manufactured goods, iron, and steel. Numerous announcements have been made about the creation of joint enterprises or bilateral projects, but it is difficult to measure their progress from afar. Nonetheless, the two countries are attempting to follow up on these projects through joint commissions, five of which have taken place since 1998, meaning that they began before Ahmadinejad became president.[36] A few concrete examples of successful deals have been reported by the press. In March 2006, Iran and Venezuela signed an agreement totaling $404.6 million for the joint construction of 10,000 homes in Venezuela within 15 months. Another agreement for the construction of 7,000 dwellings including apartments and small homes was signed on 19 December 2006 and ratified in January 2007. Furthermore, a tractor factory in the state of Bolívar, Veneirán Tractor, operates with 70 Venezuelan employees under the direction of 8 Iranian managers. The factory was inaugurated on 12 March 2005 and is slated to produce some 5,000 tractors in 2007. In July 2006, Iranian tractors produced in a joint factory were already operating in Venezuela, and the Iranian company Khodro forecasts a production of 5,000 Samand automobiles per year beginning in November 2006 in a factory near Caracas. Two months later, the two leaders announced the construction of two cement factories in the states of Monagas and Lara with support from Iran that would allow construction of housing in Venezuela. In July 2007, during Chávez's visit to Iran, 14 contracts were to have been signed for the construction of homes, injection molding, and milk treatment, and the Venezuelan president went to visit the bilateral projects in the special zone of Asalouyeh.[37] Finally, in September 2007, agreements were signed not only in the petrochemical field but also in the agricultural industry (with the creation of nine factories for corn processing) and automobile production. Additionally, during this same meeting, the two leaders signed three new agreements aimed at developing projects within the Pars Special Energy Economic Zone (PSEEZ) in Iran and the Venezuelan petrochemical industrial complex of José Antonio Anzoátegui, the first unit of the joint company Venirán.[38] The presidents of Iran and of Venezuela have often mentioned their desire to create a bilateral development fund, and this was accomplished in May 2008. Two institutions were established, the Iran-Venezuela Bank in Teheran for financing economic programs and a single joint fund located in Caracas for financing public projects as well as individuals and companies. Each institution will be launched with $1 billion as initial capital.[39] Of course, many of the projects involve the petroleum sector: Venezuela is encouraging Iran to participate in petroleum exploration in the Orinoco Belt, the country's large reserve of extra heavy crude, and Petropars has begun studies to quantify and certify the reserves in Block 7 of this zone, in collaboration with PDVSA (Petróleos de Venezuela, S. A.). The two presidents have also signed agreements to create joint ventures in order to enhance the complementarity of their economies and increase their respective autonomies. Practically speaking, Venezuela lacks technicians, particularly after the strike in 2002–03, and Iran lacks refined petroleum. In December 2006, PDVSA and Sadra America Latina, C. A. signed an agreement to form the Venezirian Oil Company, headquartered in Caracas,[40] and in January 2007, Chávez and Ahmadinejad agreed to launch the Venezuela-Irán Petroquímica Company to be located in Guiria to manufacture products derived from petroleum. Another aspect of their economic collaboration is the development of infrastructure, notably deficient in developing countries although critical to trade. For this reason, on 5 March, Venezuelan Foreign Affairs Minister Maduro ushered in a new airline linking Caracas, Damascus, and Teheran.[41]

Finally, one of the obstacles to the development of relations between developing countries is a lack of knowledge of their respective cultures. Iran and Venezuela have taken some steps to address this shortcoming. For example, they have experimented with university exchange programs, and a Memorandum of Understanding has been signed by their official press agencies, the Bolivarian News Agency and the Islamic Republic News Agency. In celebration of the anniversary of Iran's Independence Day, a play by Venezuelan Néstor Caballero, *Dados*, was premiered in Teheran in April 2006.[42]

Thus, efforts to intensify bilateral relations began even before the arrival of Ahmadinejad on the scene. The results are visible although they have not yet achieved the objectives established by the two countries, partly because of the limits inherent in their strategy to forge closer relations.

Limits to the Iran-Venezuela Relationship

A timely overlap of their tenure in office, a favorable international context, shared criticism of the United States—these are a few of the elements that have fostered and facilitated closer relations between Iran and Venezuela. It is also clear that the strengthening of the bilateral relationship has occurred at an auspicious moment internationally, which partly explains the attention it has drawn. This dependence upon the international context, however, could become a weakness in their future relations if circumstances take a less favorable turn.

Both Iran and Venezuela clearly benefit from increasing oil prices, which provide them with the financial resources to support their foreign policy objectives: they have essentially transformed their black gold into a political instrument. Nevertheless, their ability to act would be greatly reduced in the event of a drop in oil prices; this in turn would limit their ability to assert themselves globally and act on their bilateral agreements.[43] However, the current situation does not appear to be tending toward any drastic drop in the price per barrel.

It is still the case that as developing countries, Iran and Venezuela have limited financial resources to implement their foreign policy plans, which exist alongside significant pressing internal challenges. It is very costly to create ad hoc relationships because one must start from nothing, as we saw in the case of transportation. So the intrinsic limitations imposed by the two states' financial and international situations means it will take time to establish lasting bilateral relations.

Furthermore, there is a difference between words and deeds in existing relations with the United States. Relations with the world's biggest power are still pivotal to the international positioning of these two countries. Reestablishment of diplomatic ties with the United States is essential if Iran is to return to the international community. French researcher Frédéric Tellier has written: "Despite the official rhetoric, normalizing relations with Washington constitutes the Holy Grail of Iran's political life."[44] The Venezuelan president's criticisms of his American counterpart must be taken in the context of his country's dependence on the United States market, and in fact, their economic relations are not affected by his verbal attacks. In 2006, more than 50 percent of Venezuela's petroleum was exported to the United States, or 1.5 million barrels out of their total production of 2.6 million.[45] In a striking paradox, the platform from which Venezuela criticizes the president of the United States is sustained by the sale of petroleum to this same country.

In the end, opinions vary on the future of Iran-Venezuela relations. There are signs of continuity that suggest that the relationship is not about to disappear with new changes in politics, those of Iran in particular, because Chávez's outreach policy predates Ahmadinejad's arrival on the scene. Furthermore, during his trips to Teheran, the Venezuelan president meets with the Supreme Leader, who holds the true power in Iran under the constitution.[46] It is not possible to predict how a change in Venezuela's government would affect the bilateral relationship, but Chávez has not yet reached the end of his term in office. In any case, if the relationship continues, it is quite possible that it may develop in a different manner, especially in regard to the United States.

There is little doubt that Iran and Venezuela are attempting to establish a special relationship. Iran's ties to Venezuela are closer and more diversified than its relationships with other Latin American countries, and those ties have begun to bear fruit in several areas. The principles underlying their foreign policies are compatible and have fostered connections in several domains, far deeper than the media hype about the duo of Chávez and Ahmadinejad would suggest. What's more, Iran embodies the new international profile that President Chávez has sought for Venezuela, and which corresponds to his desire for internal change. The country of the Islamic revolution, Iran, is the very symbol of the policy Venezuela has been trying to implement since 1998, characterized by independence, a global role as a major oil-producer, and solidarity with other developing countries. Iran and Venezuela have chosen to become allies in the search for international recognition for their demands for reform of the international system. Toward this end they have both opted, especially since 2005 in Iran, for a strategy based on radical rhetoric, which, while it echoes the "Third World-ism" of the 1970s, also makes plain some inherent limitations for developing countries active on the world stage.

Whether the bilateral relationship between Chávez and Ahmadinejad is viable remains an open question. There are indications that it is, and some that it is not, but no one can predict what surprises electoral changes may hold in store for the relationship. In any case, the Iran-Venezuela relationship is one example of a permanent change in the structure of international relations, whereby developing countries forge new albeit fluctuating ties. This evolution cannot be ignored by anyone who wants to understand what is really going on in the world today.

Notes

1 Salgueiro, Adolfo P., "l'Asse Caracas-Teheran," in *Limes*, no. 2, February 2007, pp. 175-181.

2 Blanco, Carlos, "La política exterior de la revolución," in *Revolución y desilusión: la Venezuela de Hugo Chávez* (Madrid : Catarata, 2002), p. 193, and "Iran Seeks Links with Venezuela," in *The Guardian Unlimited*, 23 June 2006.

3 "OPEP pide a Estados Unidos cese de agresiones contra sus miembros," in *Boletines del MRE de Venezuela*, 17 November 2007.

4 "Chavez et Ahmadinejad soutiennent une baisse de production de l'OPEP," in *La Tribune*, 15 January 2007, and Espinosa, Ángeles, "Venezuela e Irán se unen al pedir para la OPEP un papel político activo," in *El País*, 18 November 2007.

5 "Venezuela participa junto con Irán y Malasía en refinería en Siria," at *Aporrea.org*, 30 October 2007.

6 "Canciller Nicolás Maduro instaló V Comisión mixta Venezuela-Irán," in *Boletines del MRE de Venezuela*, 21 April 2008. Original text: "Es una alianza para que los pequeños podamos tener derecho a la vida."

7 Thomassin, Catherine, "La place du pétrole dans la politique extérieure du Venezuela," presented at the international summer seminar on the Americas at Université Laval, 15 June 2007.

8 ALBA was launched in 2004 by Cuba and Venezuela; among its member countries are Bolivia, Cuba, Dominica, Nicaragua, and Venezuela. The project emphasizes social issues, not just economic ones, something for which the FTAA is sometimes criticized.

9 "Resumen de noticias internacionales," in *Boletines del MRE de Venezuela*, 2 July 2007.

10 "El desarrollo del eje Orinoco-Apure fue el tema central de la V Comisión mixta Venezuela-Irán," *Boletines del MRE de Venezuela*, 22 April 2008.

11 Erikson, Dan, "Ahmadinejad Finds it Warmer in Latin America," in *Los Angeles Times*, 3 October 2007.

12 "Ahmadinejad propose une alliance des 'révolutionnaires,'" in *Le Nouvel Observateur*, 16 January 2007, and "Mahmoud Ahmadinejad se dit prêt à aider la Bolivie," *IRNA*, 8 February 2007.

13 "Ahmadinejad, un invitado incómodo en Suramérica," in *El País*, 16 January 2007, and Romero, Carlos, "Venezuela : une société en mutation," in *Problèmes d'Amérique Latine*, no. 65, summer 2007, pp. 11-31.

14 According to the ECLAC database, Iran was the world's twentieth largest recipient of Brazilian exports in 2005.

15 Brun, Elodie, *Les relations entre l'Amérique du Sud et le Moyen-Orient. Un exemple de relance Sud-Sud* (Paris: L'Harmattan, 2008).

16 Klich, Ignacio, "Et le Proche-Orient fait irruption en Argentine," in *Le Monde Diplomatique*, March 2007. In 2006, Argentine courts upheld official charges of Iran's responsibility in the 18 July 1994 bombing of the Asociación Mutual

Israelita Argentina (AMIA) leaving 85 dead and 200 wounded. In spite of this, diplomatic relations were not severed.

17 "Statue of Venezuela's Founding Father Unveiled in Tehran in Presence of Chavez," at *Payvand.com*, 28 November 2004. Original text: "Las naciones iraníes y latino-americanas luchan por la libertad y alientan las revueltas anticolonialistas en los otros países."

18 Romero, Carlos, *Jugando con el globo. La política exterior de Hugo Chávez* (Caracas: Ediciones B, grupe Zeta, 2006), p. 10. Original text: "El anti-norteamericanismo se ha constitutido en una punta de lanza de la diplomacia venezolana."

19 The 444-day episode during which Iranian students held 63 US citizens captive, the majority of whom worked at the Teheran embassy.

20 "Mahmoud Ahmadinejad, révolutionnaire sud-américain," at *geostrategie.com*, 16 January 2007.

21 Ghazi, Siavosh, "Le guide suprême iranien et le président vénézuélien pourfendent les Etats-Unis," *AFP*, 1 July 2007.

22 Delpech, Thérèse, "Le Moyen-Orient de Mahmoud Ahmadinejad," in *Politique Internationale*, no. 114, winter 2007.

23 Malmund, Carlos and García Encina, Carlota, "Los actores extrarregionales en América Latina (II) : Irán," ARI no. 124/2007, Real Instituto Elcano, 26 November 2007. Original text: "Les gustan los grandes titulares."

24 Flores Victor, "Venezuela-Iran : une alliance anti-Washington," *AFP*, 17 September 2006.

25 Shifter, Michael, "In Search of Hugo Chavez," in *Foreign Affairs*, 85 (3), May-June 2006, pp. 45-59; Garrido, Alberto, *Revolución bolivariana 2005: notas* (Caracas: Alberto Garrido, 2005); and Thomassin, Catherine, "La place du pétrole dans la politique extérieure du Venezuela," presented at the international summer seminar on the Americas at Université Laval, 15 June 2007.

26 Romero, Carlos, *Jugando con el globo. La política exterior de Hugo Chávez* (Caracas: Ediciones B, grupe Zeta, 2006), p. 81.

27 "L'Iran lance sa propre chaîne d'information en langue anglaise," at *Challenges.fr*, 3 July 2007.

28 "Venezuela, Iran initial 29 accords," in *El Universal*, 22 September 2007.

29 "Ahmadinejad drague les latinos," at *geostrategie.com*, 30 January 2007.

30 Romero, Simon, "Venezuela and Iran Strengthen Ties With Caracas-to-Tehran Flight," in *The New York Times*, 3 March 2007, and "Venezuela-Iran : la coopération militaire et technique décolle," at *geostrategie.com*, 3 February 2007.

31 Pérez, Benito, "Les faux-amis du Venezuela," at risal.info, 5 July 2007.

32 "El desarrollo del eje Orinoco-Apure fue el tema central de la V Comisión mixta Venezuela-Irán," in *Boletines del MRE de Venezuela*, 22 April 2008.

33 For a detailed review of the economic relationship, please see Annexe 3 in Brun, Elodie, *Les relations entre l'Amérique du Sud et le Moyen-Orient. Un exemple de relance Sud-Sud* (Paris: L'Harmattan, 2008), pp. 183-194.

34 Malmund, Carlos and García Encina, Carlota, "Los actores extrarregionales en América Latina (II) : Irán," ARI no. 124/2007, Real Instituto Elcano, 26 November 2007.

35 For data on imports and exports, please see http://comtrade.un.org/db/default.aspx

36 Held in: Caracas in February 2002; Teheran in August 2004; Caracas in December 2005; Teheran in March 2007; and Caracas in April 2008.

37 "Iran-Venezuela Presidents Break Ground for Methanol Complex," *IRNA*, 1 July 2007.

38 "Suscritos tres nuevos documentos de cooperación mutua entre Venezuela e Irán," in *Boletines del MRE de Venezuela*, 28 September 2007.

39 "Crearán Banco Binacional Iraní-Venezolano," *ABN*, 20 May 2008.

40 "L'Iran et le Venezuela créent une société pétrolière mixte," in *Iran Focus News*, 22 December 2006.

41 Romero, Simon, "Venezuela and Iran Strengthen Ties with Caracas-to-Tehran Flight", *The New York Times*, 3 March 2007.

42 "Obra teatral 'Dados' estrenada con éxito en Teherán," in *Embavenez Irán*, 24 April 2006.

43 For example, nearly 50 percent of Venezuela's revenues come from petroleum.

44 Tellier, Frédéric, *L'heure de l'Iran* (Paris : Ellipses, 2005), p. 136.

45 Lapper, Richard, "Living with Hugo: US Policy toward Hugo Chávez's Venezuela," CFR Special Report no. 20, Council on Foreign Relations, November 2006.

46 Article 110 of the Iranian constitution states that the Leader is responsible for setting forth the general policies of the regime, and Article 122 states that the president is responsible to the Leader. See also "Hugo Chavez quitte Téhéran," *IRNA*, 31 July 2006, and "Ahmadinejad Officially Welcomes Venezuela's Chavez," *IRNA*, 1 July 2007

References

- Carlos Blanco, "La política exterior de la revolución" and "Puntos de confrontación," dans Revolución y desilusión : la Venezuela de Hugo Chávez, Madrid : Catarata, 2002, p.169-198 et p.199-232.

- Elodie Brun, Les relations entre l'Amérique du Sud et le Moyen-Orient. Un exemple de relance Sud-Sud, Paris : L'Harmattan, 2008, 200 p.

- Heinz Dieterich and Hugo Chávez Frías, Hugo Chávez : un nuevo proyecto latinoamericano, La Habana : Editorial de Ciencias Sociales, 2001, 115 p.

- Rafael Duarte Villa, "Dos etapas en la política exterior venezolana frente a Estados Unidos en el período de Hugo Chávez," Cuadernos del CENDES, année 21, n°55, janvier-avril 2004, p.21-45.

- Daniel P. Erikson, "Requiem for the Monroe Doctrine," Current History, février 2008, p.58-64.

- Alberto Garrido, Revolución bolivariana 2005: notas, Caracas : Alberto Garrido, 2005, 126 p.

- Albert O. Hirschman, Défection et prise de parole, théorie et applications, Paris : Fayard, 1995, 212 p.

- Richard Lapper, "Living with Hugo: US Policy Toward Hugo Chávez's Venezuela," rapport special n°20, Council on Foreign Relations, novembre 2006, 57 p.

- Carlos Malmund and Carlota García Encina, "Los actores extrarregionales en América Latina (II) : Irán," Real Instituto Elcano, ARI n°124/2007, 26 novembre 2007.

- Carlos Romero, "Venezuela : une société en mutation," Problèmes d'Amérique Latine, n°65, été 2007, p.11-31.

- Carlos Romero, Jugando con el globo. La política exterior de Hugo Chávez, Caracas: Ediciones B, grupe Zeta, 2006, 230 p.

- Adolfo P. Salguiero, "l'Asse Caracas-Teheran." Limes, n°2, février 2007, p.175-181 ;

- Michael Shifter, "In search of Hugo Chávez," Foreign Affairs, 85 (3), mai-juin 2006, p.45-59.

- Catherine Thomassin, "La place du pétrole dans la politique extérieure du Venezuela", travail présenté lors du séminaire international d'été sur les Amériques à l'Université de Laval, 15 juin 2007, 33 p.

-"Venezuela Iran's Best Friend ?," venezuelanalysis.com, 11 mars 2006

THE SHADOW OF IRAN IN ARGENTINA TAKES ON A SUSPICIOUS SHAPE

HUGO ALCONADA MON

The Tehran regime appears to be the primary suspect in having devised and planned two attacks: the bombing of the Israeli Embassy in Buenos Aires on March 17, 1992, and the bombing of the Argentine Jewish Mutual Association (Asociación Mutual Israelita Argentina, or AMIA) two years later, on July 18, 1994.

The Buenos Aires targets were chosen for a number of reasons. The country is home to the largest Jewish community in South America and one of the largest outside of Israel. However, there are other possible reasons, including the participation of Argentine ships in the 1991 Gulf War and the fluctuating relations that Argentine President Carlos Menem and his administration maintained with governments in the Middle East, while at the same time affirming an explicit alliance with the United States and a commitment to the defense of Israel. Clear examples of the volatility of these relationships can be seen in the pattern of contributions to his electoral campaign, the cancellation of both a sale of nuclear reactors to Syria and of the Condor missile project with Egypt, and suspension of the nuclear technology assistance that Argentina had offered Iran.

Investigations of the two attacks produced little in the way of concrete results, though they did uncover some of the alleged conspirators, material participants and local agents involved, as well as possible terrorist cells and their logistical and financial support groups in the border area known as the "Triple Frontier" between Argentina, Brazil and Paraguay. For years, the region has been the epicenter of operations for money laundering and for narcotics, arms and human trafficking, making the region a matter of continuing concern to Washington.[1]

The Attack on the Israeli Embassy

The public investigation of the Embassy attack, in which 22 people were killed and dozens more wounded, was overseen by the Supreme Court (Case S. 143). Because it affected a foreign diplomatic entity, it fell under the jurisdiction of Article 117 of the Argentine Constitution.

As recently as May of 1999—more than seven years after the attack—the Court ruled that "the attack committed against the Israeli Embassy in Argentina on March 17, 1992 was organized and carried out by the terrorist group known as Islamic Jihad, a militant arm of Hezbollah"—a finding that was confirmed by a number of reports in December of 2008 pointing to the Triple Frontier.[2]

For years, the United States had been voicing suspicions about Hezbollah and Iranian responsibility for the attacks. A month before the Court's ruling, for example, the U.S. State Department's annual report on terrorism referred to Hezbollah as having "attacked the Israeli Embassy in Argentina in 1992."

The prima facie individual suspects named by the Court as being responsible for the attack were Imad Fayez Mugniyah, aka "Mughniyeh," of Lebanon, a senior Hezbollah official and possible head of the group's intelligence division, and Samuel Salman el-Reda, a Colombian national of Lebanese descent married to an Argentine national, who was suspected of being the local coordinator. These suspicions of Iran and Hezbollah were shared by the Israeli government.[3]

Mugniyah was on the FBI's list of 24 most wanted terrorists, until his assassination by an anonymously placed car bomb in Damascus, in February of 2008,[4] and he was also wanted for participating in three kidnappings and two attacks in the 1980s, in which more than 310 American citizens in Lebanon were killed.

According to evidence compiled by the Court, Mugniyah was in Argentina in July of 1994 just before the second attack (on the AMIA) and met there with his local contacts, leaving the country some days before the actual attack. He was later assassinated in Syria in February of 2008.[5]

In March of 2008, on the 16th anniversary of the attack, Minister of Justice and Security, Aníbal Fernández and his Israeli counterpart Avi Dijter blamed the attack on "international terrorism," although it was the Israeli official who singled out Hezbollah and the "deranged leaders of the Iranian government," pointing out that the Argentine courts had linked Iran with the Embassy and AMIA attacks. Referring to that finding, he added, "The conclusion is specific, courageous and intelligent."[6]

The AMIA Attack

In addition to the Court's investigation of the Israeli Embassy attack, there is information from the investigation of the attack on the AMIA, which resulted in 85 deaths and dozens more injured. This incident provides a clear example of how Argentina's justice system actually operates.

The investigation of the attacks was directed by federal judge Juan José Galeano, in conjunction with federal prosecutors Eamon Mullen and José Barbaccia, who focused their attention on the "local connections" involved in the incidents. Today, it is the investigators who are being investigated.

Any results-based assessment of Galeano's performance must begin with the fact that after ten years of work, he was unable to charge a single suspect. The investigation was annulled. Galeano was dismissed by the Council of Magistrates and currently stands accused of a number of crimes.

From the early stages of his investigation, Galeano focused on a mechanic by the name of Carlos Telleldín, from whom the white Renault Trafic van used in the attack was purchased, as well as on several police officers, including Juan José Ribelli—identified by Galeano as the "local connection"—who was held in prison for ten years.

Galeano's performance—along with that of government officials, police officers, and even directors of major local Jewish organizations such as the AMIA and the Delegation of Argentine Jewish Associations (Delegación de Asociaciones Israelitas Argentinas, or DAIA)—became the subject of sharp criticism. Eventually, a second criminal investigation was undertaken to determine whether, among other possible improprieties, political figures had conspired to conceal the attack. As of August 2000, this investigation was overseen by federal judge Claudio Bonadío.

Nevertheless, Galeano remained at the forefront of the AMIA case—a case in which suspicions about the role of Iran and Hezbollah first surfaced in the weeks immediately following the attack.[7] Only nine years later, however, in March, May, and August of 2003, did Galeano request international warrants for a dozen former Iranian officials and diplomats and one Lebanese suspect, alleging that they were linked to the attack.

Galeano set his sights on the Iranian ambassador in Buenos Aires, Hadi Soleimanpour, his fellow diplomat Ahmad Reza Asghari, former cultural affairs attaché Mohsen Rabbani, former Intelligence Minister Ali Fallahian, and Barat Ali Balesh Abadi, who was a courier working for Iranian intelligence.[8] Galeano's warrant also named Hezbollah's special operations officer Imad Mughniyah (a Lebanese national who was also wanted by the United States), Ali Akhbar Parvarash, who was Education Minister at the time of the terrorist attack, and diplomatic couriers Hossein Ali Tabrizi, Masoud Amiri, Seyed Yousef Arabi, Ahmad Alamolhoda, Mahmoud Monzavizadeh and Saied Baghban.

The investigation collapsed on September 2, 2004, however, when the Third *Tribunal Oral Federal* (Federal Trial Court) dismissed the charges against Galeano's suspects and ordered an acquittal of Carlos Telleldín and four Buenos Aires police officers. A month after the decision, the Court issued a harsh rebuke of Galeano, accusing him of "architectural construction" in building his case, and of falsifying evidence against the imprisoned police officers.[9] The Court concluded that "as a result of the numerous verifiable irregularities, we have established that Judge Galeano sought to construct an incriminating hypothesis that would meet the logical demands of society while at the same time satisfying the shadowy interests of unscrupulous elements within the government. He abandoned the pursuit of truth and engaged in behavior contrary to the law, behavior in which he had the collaboration, by action or by omission, of several bodies within the three branches of government that provided him political support and cover for his irregular and unlawful acts."

According to the Court's presiding judges—Gerardo Larrambebere, Miguel Pons and Guillermo Gordo—Galeano paid Carlos Telleldín 400,000 pesos[10] in exchange for his testimony regarding the person to whom he had delivered the van used in the car-bomb attack. He is also alleged to have pressured witnesses and fabricated evidence. The funds for Telleldín's bribe came from the State Secretary of Intelligence, or

SIDE, which was then under the control of Menem supporter Hugo Anzorreguy.[11]

An unforeseen consequence of this failure was that it reinforced Iran's argument that Argentina's failure to identify the terrorists behind the attack resulted from "judicial corruption," rather than from any lack of cooperation on the part of Iran, pointing to what it called "Zionist lobbies" and their "unfounded accusations" and "irrational complaints."[12]

Just days after the Court's ruling, the Lebanese Ambassador to Argentina, Hicham Hamdan, also joined the fray, downplaying the accusations against Hezbollah, while maintaining that "SIDE's information actually comes from Mossad."[13]

The failure in the case had far more serious consequences than the Lebanese and Iranian declarations, however. In September of 2005, it caused INTERPOL to revoke the warrants for the Iranian suspects who—thanks to Galeano—had been cleared.[14]

After the harsh rebuke handed down by the Court, Galeano tendered his resignation, which was refused by President Néstor Kirchner. On August 3, 2005, the Council of Magistrates dismissed him, and in May of 2006, the nation's highest criminal court, the *Cámara de Casación* (Court of Appeals), upheld the ruling dismissing the charges, and emphasized the inefficiency of the intelligence services and the lack of specific laws on terrorism investigations.[15]

The Second Investigation: "AMIA II"

When the Court dealt the final blow to Galeano's investigation, the case was handed over to Judge Rodolfo Canicoba Corral, who in turn passed it on to the Special Investigative Unit (UEI)[16] created by the Ministry of Justice in 2000 specifically for this case. The unit was headed by attorneys Alberto Nisman and Marcelo Martínez Burgos.

Eventually, in November of 2005, the Federal Court removed Judge Bonadío from the case before he began his investigation on whether Galeano, former prosecutors Mullen and Barbaccia, and former head of SIDE, Anzorreguy, among other officials, had committed any crimes or misconduct. This ruling came from a different federal judge, Ariel Lijo.

Unlike Bonadío, who achieved little in his five years on the case, Lijo, by September of 2006, was able to bring multiple charges against Galeano, Anzorreguy, the former head of the DAIA, Rubén Beraja, former public prosecutors Mullen and Barbaccia, several police officers, and the original suspect in the case, Carlos Telleldín, among others.[17]

In July of 2007, the Federal Court confirmed the charges against Galeano, Anzorreguy, Beraja, Telleldín, the latter's wife, and her lawyer, and established grounds for serious charges against prosecutors Mullen and Barbaccia. However, it went even further, ordering that investigations against former President Menem and his Minister of the Interior, Carlos Corach, be expanded.[18]

On May 22, 2008, in Judge Lijo's court, public prosecutor Nisman requested an arrest warrant for former President Menem, his brother—the former chief of SIDE—Munir Menem, Anzorreguy, and Galeano for hindering the prosecution of Alberto Jacinth Kanore Edul of Syria.

Evidence indicated that on July 10, 1994, the day on which the white Renault Trafic van was delivered to the terrorists, Kanore Edul placed a phone call to the van's owner, Telleldín. Also in Edul's address book was the phone number of Mohsen Rabbani, the former cultural affairs attaché at the Iranian Embassy in Buenos Aires. One of Galeano's former colleagues on the case, Claudios Lifshitz, testified under oath that the case against Kaqnore Edul was never pursued because Munir Menem had called Galeano, ordering him to abort the investigation.

INTERPOL—A Blunder and a New Order

In October of 2006, two years and a month after the Federal Trial Court dismissed the charges filed by Galeano, Nisman renewed the accusation that the Iranian government was involved in the attack on AMIA. He accused Iran of making the decision during a meeting of the Special Affairs Committee in the city of Mashhad on August 14th, 1993.[19] His accusation was supported by cross-referencing over 300 million phone calls, as well as by witness testimony and intelligence reports.[20]

According to the Public Prosecutor's office, the attack began to take shape when the van provided by Carlos Telleldín was equipped with a car bomb, driven by a Lebanese man named Ibrahim Berro. The terrorists who collaborated on planning the attack allegedly entered Argentina on July 1st at the Ezeiza International Airport, leaving the day of the attack, July 18th, via the Jorge Newbery Metropolitan Airport.

It was clear to the prosecutors involved in the AMIA case—as had been demonstrated by the Supreme Court in its investigation of the 1992 attack on the Israeli Embassy—that "Hezbollah terrorist cells in the Triple Frontier" had been operating, and that, in July of 1994, at least two phone calls were placed from a mosque in that region to relatives of Ibrahim Berro.

A couple weeks later, Federal Judge Rodolfo Canicoba Corral categorized the attack as a crime against humanity—a charge that has no statute of limitations—and issued new international arrest warrants for nine suspects.

In March of 2007, INTERPOL decided to publish the advisories requested by the Argentinean National Central Bureau (NCB) for Hezbollah operative Imad Fayez Moughnieh, former Iranian Intelligence Minister Ali Fallahian, cultural affairs attaché Mohsen Rabbani, third secretary of the Iranian embassy in Buenos Aires, Ahmad Reza Asghari, former ambassador Hadi Soleimanpour, and Ahmad Vahidi and Mohsen Rezai, both former officers in Iran's Islamic Revolutionary Guards Corps (IRGC).

Interpol refused to go after three key suspects: the former Iranian President and then head of the Expediency Discernment Council of Iran, Alí Hashemi Rafsanjani; former Minister of Foreign Affairs, Alí Akbar Velayati; and the former Iranian Ambassador in Buenos Aires, Hadi Soleimanpour.[21]

Iran appealed INTERPOL's decision, and the diplomatic tensions between Buenos Aires and Tehran worsened to the point that, in September of 2007, Argentine President Néstor Kirchner made a formal protest before the United Nations General Assembly.[22] Two months later, in November of that same year, INTERPOL reaffirmed its decision. By a vote of 78 in favor and 14 opposed, with 26 abstentions, it authorized the issuing of immediate arrest warrants for five former officials from Iran and one Lebanese national.[23] The suspects named in the warrant included the same suspects the NCB had named in March of 2007.

The advances made in the investigations driven by the prosecutor Nisman and the judges Canicobra Corral and Lijo earned the endorsement of a number of international Jewish organizations such as the American Jewish Committee,[24] although differences remained between local entities. Argentina's push for justice also garnered explicit support from the White House[25] and the United States Congress,[26] although Iran continued to unequivocally reject Argentina's assertions. Barely 24 hours after INTERPOL's latest decision, Iran declared it "unfounded" and "unacceptable," and stated that bilateral cooperation had failed because of "the influence of Argentine Zionists."[27]

Tehran cranked up the tension another notch on November 13th, 2007, when an Iranian judge ordered the appearance of five Argentine nationals accused of making untrue allegations: former minister Corach, former judge Galeano, former prosecutors Mullen and Barbaccia, and the former president of DAIA, Rubén Beraja.[28]

Washington, D.C.

Meanwhile, in 1999, because of the lack of developments and the controversial methods employed during Judge Galeano's investigation, the group Active Memory—comprised of family members of victims of the AMIA attack—gathered before the Inter-American Commission on Human Rights (IACHR) to protest the Argentine judicial system which, for years, had ignored their demands. The protests appeared to change when Néstor Kirchner took office. The State yielded to Active Memory's demands in March of 2005,[29] admitting its responsibility for the lack of progress in the AMIA attack case, and committing to building an extensive list of new measures and reforms.

Until recently, however, that commitment lacked any "concrete actions on the part of the State, which has demonstrated its inability to fulfill the commitments it makes," according to a statement released by Active Memory in conjunction with the Center for Legal and Social Studies (CELS) and the Center for Justice and International Law (CEJIL).[30] Active Memory has also been working, along with American legal efforts, since August of 2006, to declassify CIA and FBI documents pertaining to the attack.

Meanwhile, in Washington, D.C., U.S. District Judge Ellen Segal Huvelle held Iran liable for the attack on Israel's embassy in Argentina, which killed 29 people, and ordered the Iranian government to pay US$ 33 million to the family of U.S.-born Israeli diplomat David Ben-Rafael, one of 22 victims of the attack. According to the Judge, the attack was only possible thanks to "material support from the Ministry of Information and Security of Iran."[31]

The Relationship with Iran

The majority of Argentine citizens believe that Iran participated either directly or indirectly in the attacks of 1992 and 1994, despite the controversies that surrounded both investigations and the skepticism that continues to linger. Even so, it is important to note that the regime in Tehran has slightly more favorable ratings in Argentina than it has had, for years, in the United States. According to the most recent Pew Research Center's Global Attitudes Project,[32] 52 percent of Argentine citizens surveyed have a negative opinion of Iran, compared with 62 percent of Americans, even though the percentage of Argentines who have a favorable opinion of Tehran (10 percent) is lower than corresponding public opinion in the largest military and political power on the planet (22 percent). It should also be pointed out that Iran's unfavorable rating among Argentines is lower than in other Latin American countries (in Mexico, the figure is 56 percent, in Brazil, 69 percent), despite the fact that Buenos Aires suffered two attacks unparalleled in the rest of the hemisphere.[33]

The chasm between Argentina and Iran grew wider in November of 2006, when Kirchner fired his long-time point man Luis D'Elía who, after returning from a trip to Iran, criticized the Argentine judicial system, decrying its accusations against Tehran as "deeply contaminated" by "information provided by the intelligence services" of the United States and Israel, whose common objective was to "internationally isolate" Iran for "facilitating anti-American and anti-Israeli military aggression."[34] D'Elía's comments would have been little more than anecdotes were it not for the social activist's relationship with Cristina Fernández de Kirchner, who happened to be the wife of the President. In succeeding months, the talking points became a spearhead—a governmental "collision force," according to the opposition—with D'Elía even sharing the public stage with the First Lady from time to time.

Effects and Consequences

As this brief review has shown, 16 years after the first attack and 14 years after the second, both investigations are still far from complete. The parties responsible have not been brought to justice, while the victims and their families continue their tug-of-war with the Argentine government in an attempt to have their demands met. In spite of all the steps being made by the Kirchner administration and the advances made in the investigation during his mandate, there are still unfulfilled commitments from the agreement signed with the group Active Memory before the Inter-American Commission on Human Rights, in March 2005. Moreover, there is lingering concern that the attacks exposed the inability of the Argentine Government to pursue justice, when investigators and prosecutors themselves perpetrate fraud and cover-ups, sacrificing the "means" (respect for the law) in favor of achieving acceptable "ends," ultimately provoking consequences opposite to those being sought.

Ironically and lamentably, the attacks—and the flawed investigations—lend credence to all manner of conspiracy theories. These include questions about whether the Renault van was actually involved in the AMAI attack. ("Could it have been an explosion within the building?" and "Did AMIA orchestrate an attack upon itself?" are some of the questions challenging the standard theory.) Some conspiracy theorists even question the participation of terrorist cells—a reaction that, after what occurred in the United States and elsewhere in the wake of the September 11th attacks, seem an inherent part of human nature. These conspiracy theories are exacerbated by the backing that Iran receives from radical, left-wing fringe groups in Argentina—such as Quebracho, the Santucho's Workers' Revolutionary Party, and the Teresa Rodríguez Movement—or from the Union of Muslim Women and the Islamic Arabic Association of Argentina.

Nevertheless, the attacks of 1992 and 1994 had a series of what might be termed "positive" effects in Argentina:

- They encouraged security and intelligence forces to focus greater attention on the so-called "Triple Frontier" and to treat it as a strategic, lawless and sensitive area—the location where the attacks were most likely planned and developed.

- They raised awareness in Argentine society about the country's vulnerability to international terrorism, despite the fact that it is geographically distant from the Middle East, Europe, and the United States. This heightened awareness can be seen in the widespread fear of a third attack that existed, and continues to exist, across Argentina.

- They forced (over a period of years) the implementation of a series of measures to improve the Government's preparedness for an attack, although no federal attack response program has yet been established.

- They accelerated (also over a number of years) the demise of the Menem administration, some of whose members were accused of promoting impunity for the perpetrators of the attacks, a circumstance that forced the subsequent government—at least in terms of its public position—to allow, and even encourage, expanded investigations.

Notes

1 For more information, see: http://www.whitehouse.gov/nsc/waronterror/2006/sectionVI.html, http://www.state.gov/s/ct/rls/crt/2007/103710.htm#Tri-Border_Area, http://www.treas.gov/press/releases/hp190.htm, http://www.loc.gov/rr/frd/pdf-files/TerrOrgCrime_TBA.pdf, http://paraguay.usembassy.gov/tri-border_area.html, http://www.army.mil/professionalwriting/volumes/volume3/january_2005/1_05_4.html

2 See: http://www.csjn.gov.ar/documentos/cfal3/ver_fallos.jsp?id=0&fori=ORS00143-243

3 See: http://buenosaires.mfa.gov.il/mfm/web/main/document.asp?SubjectID=34001&MissionID=1&LanguageID=501&StatusID=0&DocumentID=-1

4 See: http://www.fbi.gov/terrorinfo/counterrorism/tsc.htm

5 See: http://www.elmundo.es/elmundo/2008/02/13/obituarios/1202920605.html

6 On this occasion, Israel's Ambassador to Argentina, Rafael Eldad, combined elegies with complaints: "We see goodwill gestures in this Government. But the local connection remains to be clarified," he stated, adding that "No one went to prison, nor has anyone been indicted."

7 As early as August of 1994, a former diplomat and Iranian agent of doubtful reliability, Manoucher Moatamer, stated that Iranian officials were involved in planning the Embassy and AMIA attacks. To that early testimony, which Galeano obtained in Caracas, Moatamer added a second testimonial in November 1997, in Los Angeles (United States), where he resides as a political refugee. This involved more than 30 hours of statements, for which supporting documents were provided.

8 Galeano concluded that the AMIA building was chosen as the site for the attack because many activities in support of the Jewish community are organized and/or take place there. Additionally, it has a certain institutional importance and is centrally located.

9 See: http://www2.jus.gov.ar/Amia/sentencia.htm

10 The equivalent of US$ 400,000, given the fixed exchange rate between the dollar and the peso that was in effect at the time.

11 Both Anzorreguy and the Minister of the Interior, Carlos Corach, were among the former State officials singled out by the Court: "After the attack occurred, the political branch of government, national officials, and the City of Buenos Aires alternated between improper interference in the official proceedings, indifference, and a lack of commitment to the cause of truth and justice."

12 See: http://www2.irna.ir/occasion/amia/index.html

13 Hamdan went even further: "Hezbollah's participation in the attack against AMIA is a theory that damages the relationship between Lebanon and Argentina," he said—a theory reinforced "by the political motives of Israel and the United States."

14 See: http://www.interpol.int/public/ICPO/PressReleases/PR2005/PR200541Es.asp

15 According to the Court, "the investigation was characterized by informal interviews, clandestine filming, illegal wiretaps, resolutions without proper probative foundation, the creation of files with intent to conceal evidence, anonymous testimony, witness tampering, and false allegations."

16 See: http://www2.jus.gov.ar/AMIA/UEI.htm

17 Lijo charged Galeano with the false imprisonment of four former Buenos Aires police officers, repeated coercion of prisoners and witnesses, fabrication of evidence, and embezzlement of public funds. Additionally, Galeano was linked with the seizure of 3 million pesos.

18 It is also notable that the first person convicted and sentenced for the attack on AMIA was the Federal Police commissioner Carlos Castañeda, for destroying or losing (among other evidence) 68 taped recordings of telephone calls made by Telleldín, undeveloped rolls of film, video tapes, and 13 computer disks seized during a search of Telleldín's home.

19 See: http://www.lanacion.com.ar/nota.asp?nota_id=852540 and http://www.clarin.com/diario/2006/10/26/elpais/p-01010.htm

20 "We have determined that the decision to attack AMIA was made in August of 1993 at the highest levels of the Iranian Government, which then delegated the organizing and execution of the attack to Hezbollah," maintained Nisman, pointing to Mohsen Rabbani, third secretary of the Iranian Embassy in Buenos Aires, as the bridge between Hezbollah and the so-called "local connection."

21 See: http://www.interpol.int/public/ICPO/PressReleases/PR2007/PR200705.asp

22 Kirchner accused Iran of not offering "all of the necessary cooperation" with the Argentine judicial system by refusing to turn over the suspects for questioning. "The only objective the Government has is solving this crime. We are asking Iran to comply. Nothing more, but also nothing less." See: http://www.casarosada.gov.ar/index.php?option=com_content&task=view&id=1231

23 See: http://www.interpol.int/Public/ICPO/PressReleases/PR2007/PR200754.asp

24 See: http://www.ajcespanol.org/site/apps/nlnet/content2.aspx?c=hwKTJeNZJtF&b=1034015&ct=2356069

25 See: http://www.whitehouse.gov/news/releases/2006/11/20061111-2.html

26 See: House of Representatives Resolution 188, approved on July 30th, 2007.

27 "In order to ascertain the truth about the attack, and to identify those truly guilty, Tehran suggested some time ago the creation of a joint legal commission," said Iranian Foreign Affairs spokesman Seyed Mohammad Ali Hosseini, but "the judicial system, influenced by Argentine Zionists, has refused to extend any sort of cooperation to the Iranian Republic."

28 That confrontational dynamic continues. Early in 2008, Iran's Attorney General, Ghorban Ali Dorri Najafabadi, stated that he would "prosecute, through local and international judicial institutions, any Argentine responsible for making accusations against Iranian citizens."

29 See: http://www2.jus.gov.ar/AMIA/reconocimiento.pdf

30 The commitments included putting in place a "contingency plan" for future emergencies, and the digitization of immigration documents. See: http://www.memoriaactiva.com/OEA_octubre2006.htm

31 See: http://dc.findacase.com/research/wfrmDocViewer.aspx/xq/fac.%5CFDCT%5CDDC%5C2008%5C20080225_0000146.DDC.htm/qx

32 See: http://pewglobal.org/reports/pdf/260.pdf

33 Meanwhile, bilateral trade relations between Argentina and Iran are all but nonexistent, following the gradual growth seen between 1999, when Argentina's exports to Iran totaled US$ 155 million, and 2001, when the figure reached US$ 417 million—more than the country's exports to the United Kingdom (US$ 291 million), Venezuela (US$ 235 million) or France (US$ 257 million), to name but a few examples. The trend reversed itself in 2002, due in no small part to Néstor Kirchner becoming President. Under his administration, exports to Iran fell to US$ 47 million in 2003 and to US$ 1 million in 2004. In 2005, figures were too low to be reported.

34 In April of 2007, D'Elía hit harder. He called for an investigation into "the Israeli right" in connection with the two attacks, and speculated that those involved could be "the same ones who killed [Yitzhak] Rabin or sabotaged the peace accords at Camp David."

IRANIAN-NICARAGUAN RELATIONS UNDER THE SANDINISTA GOVERNMENT: Rhetoric or Anti-Establishment Foreign Policy?

Félix Maradiaga
Javier Meléndez

Introduction

The titles of the chapters in this book suggest a continuing thread of coincidences in Iran's bilateral relations with Bolivia, Ecuador and Nicaragua. These relationships share, at a minimum, a disdain for the establishment, expressed in their clearly anti-American rhetoric—rhetoric, however, that has not translated into bilateral projects of the scope implied by President Mahmoud Ahmadinejad's comments during his visit to the region. A second common feature of the relationship between these Latin American governments and Iran is the role that President Hugo Chávez and his administration play in their increasingly close ties with the Islamic Republic. Indeed, because of that closeness, any analysis of these bilateral relationships must view them as part of a triangle, in which Caracas is the third vertex. In the case of Nicaragua, some observers consider the relationship with Iran to be one of mere rhetoric; others believe that Nicaragua has made a high-stakes wager, placing it in an unnecessarily disadvantageous geopolitical position.

This book is an important step toward providing a balanced, unbiased analysis of the true scope of relations between Bolivia, Nicaragua, Ecuador, and Venezuela. This chapter will examine studies of Nicaragua's foreign policy carried out by the Institute for Strategic Studies and Public Policy (Instituto de Estudios Estratégicos y Políticas Públicas, or IEEPP) since President Daniel Ortega regained power, while noting the limitations of the task, given the dearth of official sources of data. The IEEPP considers it important for Nicaragua, as a developing nation, to make cooperative South-South relations an important element of its foreign policy. Given this priority—along with Nicaragua's strong dependence on hydrocarbons—it is not surprising that it should seek to strengthen its relationship with one of the world's major oil producers. Indeed, non-traditional bilateral relationships, such as that between Iran and Nicaragua, are a major trend in contemporary international relations. Thus, merely in terms of national priorities, there is no reason to be suspicious of the relationship. Nevertheless, cultivating relations with a nation that has been sanctioned by the United Nations for an ideologically motivated lack of transparency in respect to the Nuclear Non-Proliferation Treaty—and to do so within the framework of an anti-establishment foreign policy—provokes concern among former foreign affairs ministers and independent experts, as will be detailed below.

The Rise of Ortega and His View of Relations with Iran

Daniel Ortega Saavedra regained the Presidency of the Republic of Nicaragua after sixteen years of governing "from below." Although he left the government in 1990, he never lost his power. The agreement Ortega signed in 1999 with the leader of the opposition party, Arnoldo Alemán, allowed him to gain important footholds within the different branches of government. All that remained to formally make him Chief Executive was a victory at the polls, which became a reality on November 5, 2007. This was the state of Nicaragua's democratic system on January 10, 2008, when Ortega became president, having garnered 38 percent of the national vote—with the other sixty-two percent divided among the four other candidates. Ortega prevailed with the lowest margin of victory of any Nicaraguan president in the last twenty years.[1]

Nicaragua's position on the 2006 Economist Intelligence Unit's Democracy Index was 5.68, on a scale of one to ten, placing it 89th among the 167 countries evaluated and making it, according to *The Economist*, a "hybrid regime." The other three nations in the Americas that fell in this category were Ecuador, Venezuela and Haiti.[2]

These results are closely aligned with a study conducted by the Latin American Democratic Development Index (Indice de Desarrollo Democrático de América Latina, or IDD), in conjunction with the

Konrad Adenauer Foundation, examining democratic behavior on the part of the 18 Ibero-American nations (excluding Cuba). For 2006, the IDD regional average was 5.063, representing a mid-range level of democratic development and a slight increase over the 2005 figure of 4.842.[3] In this index, a rating below five points signifies "low democratic development." Nicaragua rated a score of 3.151, with only Venezuela, Bolivia and Ecuador ranking lower.

During his electoral campaign, Ortega was the monologue candidate. Never laying out the details or viability of his governance proposals, he declined all offers to participate in debates and never responded to questions from the press—unprecedented behavior in a Nicaraguan presidential campaign. Studying or attempting to predict President Ortega's course of action in domestic and foreign policy is therefore extremely challenging for analysts and for government observers. The task is further complicated by the lack of transparency and the low level of public access to information in Nicaragua. The IEEPP has been particularly concerned with monitoring the government's proposals and any concrete foreign policy plans. Thus, employing the same procedures used in other fields, such as national security and budgetary issues, we have attempted to speak with leading figures involved in developing and implementing those plans—attempts that, unfortunately, have proved futile.

Nevertheless, international cooperation and efforts to foster conditions that would bring down the high cost of oil were appealing themes for a presidential campaign, and such a campaign has its logic in a country where international cooperation has averaged over US$ 550 million annually for the past 17 years.[4] Indeed, the November 2006 election took place against a backdrop of national energy rationing resulting from increasing oil prices, a circumstance that candidate Ortega used to his advantage, emphasizing Nicaragua's proximity to Venezuela, the country's main oil supplier. From 2002 to 2003, the country's oil bill increased nearly 29.4 percent, but this was followed by a drop to 22.4 percent from 2003 to 2004.

In 2004-2005, oil prices per barrel increased by more than US $15, causing the cost of oil imports to rise almost thirty-five percent and making the prospect of more favorable energy policies, promoted by a new administration, extremely attractive to the electorate. From 2006 to 2007, the price of oil increased by a little less than US $10, raising the country's oil bill by more than twenty-seven percent. Finally, with a US$ 6 rise in the price of a barrel of crude between 2006 and 2007, there was a twenty-one percent increase in the cost of imports. In 2008, oil prices reached an all-time-high price of US$147,[5] negatively affecting the balance of payment and delivering a sharp blow to household economies in the form of inflation.

Unlike the rest of Central America, Nicaragua (as the table below shows) has been unable to reduce its dependency on oil for the production of electric power over the past sixteen years.[6]

Although this situation might well justify establishing bilateral relations with OPEC nations, the bilateral energy agenda with Iran, as will be seen, has not, to date, yielded the predicted results, leaving many to wonder about the pragmatic rationale for maintaining relations with the Islamic nation.

Revolutionary Foreign Policy?

Although, as noted earlier, there is a lack of official documentation, it seems clear that the relationship between President Ortega's administra-

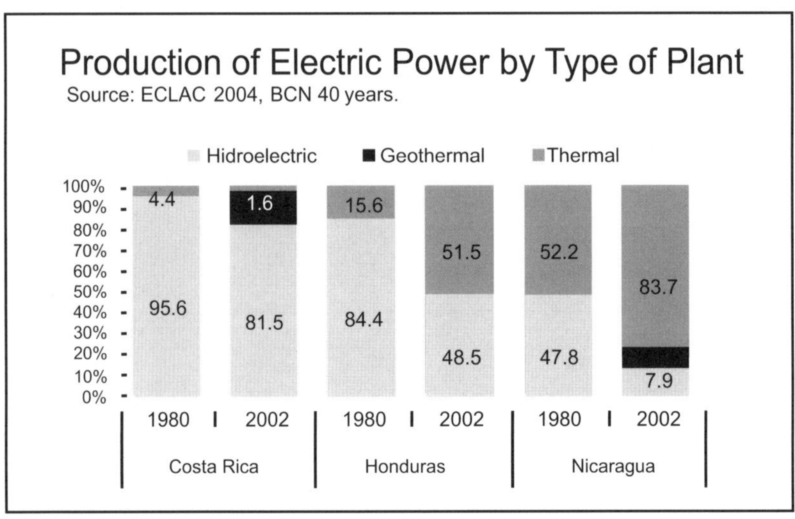

tion and the Iranian government—regardless of its potential economic significance and the Sandinista government's expectations of Iranian support for large energy projects—must be viewed as reflecting a deeply ideological perspective, with President Ortega assuming the position of a belligerent leader of international stature taking on a common regional and international cause, namely, weakening the hegemony of the United States in Latin America.

The Vision of a Revolutionary Foreign Policy

Throughout Nicaragua's history as an independent nation, its foreign policy has been dependent on, and aligned with, major centers of power and allied nations. Daniel Ortega's return to power did not represent a deviation from this course, but merely a reorientation with regard to countries that depend upon, or have recently aligned themselves with, Nicaragua. Notably, a mere hour and a half after taking office, President Ortega was awaiting the arrival of Venezuelan President Hugo Chávez. This sent a clear message about the administration's foreign policy priorities. Caracas became, from that moment forward, a central point of reference for the new government.

Despite the absence of a single public document outlining even the most general aspects of President Ortega's foreign policy, a number of events shed light on the direction in which the country's foreign policy is headed.

Upon taking office, Ortega indicated that he was inclined to maintain respectful relations with the United States, a sentiment returned by the United States, which expressed an interest in maintaining a positive and constructive relationship. However, throughout President Ortega's first year in office, his rhetoric was openly and systematically hostile to the United States. Moreover, at no point has Ortega indicated that he viewed a strategic relationship with the United States as important to Nicaragua, despite the large number of Nicaraguans living and working in the United States and the vital role they play in the Nicaraguan economy.

During his first year in office, Ortega, as part of his foreign policy, called for a "democratization" of the international system to combat the hegemony of the United States, and urged Latin Americans to unite in their efforts and capacities to fight poverty and underdevelopment. In a move not unrelated to this, he continued a rhetoric that cast himself as a "revolutionary," while joining in the anti-imperialist political and ideological vision and project known as "21st Century Socialism," promoted by his principal economic sponsor, President Hugo Chávez of Venezuela.

Despite Ortega's talk of expanding and diversifying Nicaragua's international relations, his practice has been confined to establishing or recasting existing ties within Chávez's "partnership club." Thus, not only are Ortega and Chávez allies, they also have a nearly identical roster of friends, both within the Hemisphere and beyond (Cuba, Bolivia, Ecuador, Iran, Libya, North Korea, etc.). All are united by a single common denominator: strong anti-American sentiment.

This set of circumstances binds Nicaragua's foreign policy—and therefore its fate—to actions undertaken by the other countries that are part of President Ortega's chosen group of allies, with Venezuela clearly topping the list.

Nicaragua's foreign policy also reflects President Ortega's "personalistic" style of governance—a quality evident in the conspicuousness and extravagance with which the chief executive, in a direct and single-handed approach, conducts international relations. Much of Ortega's strategy for constructing a wide-ranging network of strategic alliances with countries that are clearly adversaries of the United States—along with similarly notable efforts by the Ministry of Foreign Affairs—seems to be directed at undermining Nicaragua's cooperation and trade policies vis-à-vis its powerful North American neighbor (and principal trading partner), forged by Nicaragua's three previous administrations. Ortega also began a process designed to increase partisanship in Nicaragua's Foreign Service, returning diplomats and civil servants from the 1980s to Nicaraguan embassies around the globe and to strategic posts in the Ministry of Foreign Affairs.

According to a report by the IEEPP covering the period from September through December of 2007, Nicaragua's Foreign Policy during Ortega's first year in office featured an excessive degree of alignment with two emerging oil powers—Venezuela and Iran. This resulted in neglecting—and showing contempt for—relations with trade blocks important to Nicaragua's economy and to ongoing cooperation programs, while also affecting the tone of diplomatic relations with a number of countries such as Spain and certain Latin American nations.

Iran: A New Source of Ideological Cooperation for Nicaragua?

On January 13, 2007, a mere three days after taking office, President Ortega made a personal appearance at Managua's international airport to welcome Iranian President Mahmoud Ahmadinejad. This initial encounter between Ortega and the head of the Iranian government underlined what would become two fundamental aspects of Nicaraguan foreign policy: profoundly anti-American rhetoric, and subordination to President Hugo Chávez's ideology and oil policies. At President Ortega's inauguration several days before the encounter, Ahmadinejad's Deputy Foreign Minister for European and American Affairs, Saeed Jalili, announced that the governments of Nicaragua and Iran would sign major agreements to stimulate growth in industry, agriculture, and electric power. He specified that the agreements could include the development of agricultural machinery and plants to manufacture buses and automobiles for the regional market. The agreements also included provisions for the construction of new cement factories, ports and power plants in Nicaragua.[7]

During Ahmadinejad's visit, both Iranian and Nicaraguan officials announced the reopening of the Iranian Embassy in Managua and the Nicaraguan Embassy in Tehran. Nicaraguan political analysts, at the time, already detected a link between this new spirit of cooperation and the Iranian Government's interest in obtaining diplomatic support from Nicaragua in the United Nations.[8]

Follow-up to the Cooperative Agreements

On April 21, 2007, three months after President Ahmadinejad's visit to Nicaragua, Iran's Foreign Minister, Manoucher Motakki, visited Nicaragua to "formalize" the agreements that the presidents of the two countries had reached on January 14. According to the main Nicaraguan newspapers, the reason for the visit was both to follow through with the signing of the agreements and to identify Nicaraguan agricultural products for importation to Iran. The Iranian delegation took the opportunity to reiterate the two countries' plans for generating hydroelectric energy in Nicaragua, which were to include the construction of a damn and a hydroelectric plant in central Nicaragua.

During Motakki's visit, President Ortega publicly declared his support for the Republic of Iran's pursuit of nuclear energy for peaceful purposes, thereby taking up common cause with Iran against the resolution passed on March 24, 2007 by the United Nations Security Council,[9] demanding that Iran end its uranium enrichment activities and suspend construction of a heavy-water reactor. The resolution requested that Iran provide clarification regarding the International Atomic Energy Agency's doubts about the veracity of Iran's claim that it was pursuing nuclear energy for peaceful purposes.[10] The day after President Ortega expressed his support for Iran, historian and diplomat Aldo Díaz Lacayo (whose work strongly influences Ortega's foreign policy views), declared that the sanctions against Iran were geopolitically motivated and were intended to force Iran to negotiate with the West. To this, he added the theory that—far from being a threat—Iran was a nation that ensured peace and stability in the Middle East. Mr. Lacayo's statements lent support to the idea that the Ortega administration, from the beginning, had a clear and explicit policy of strengthening Iran's relations with Latin America, designed to serve as a base from which to oppose American hegemony in the region.

More Promises of Cooperation

On June 10, 2007, President Ortega visited the Islamic Republic of Iran for the first time. The purpose of the visit was to formalize agreements that several earlier Iranian delegations to Managua had identified and signed with the Sandinista government. The media reported widely on Ortega's statements during his visit to Tehran in which he called for establishing a new world order and supplanting capitalism and imperialism.[11]

On this occasion, the presidents of both nations reiterated their commitment to cooperation and exchange in a variety of areas intended to benefit the Nicaraguan economy. Iran's Director for Latin American Foreign Policy, speaking on behalf of the foreign ministry, also indicated that, in addition to initiating an economic partnership with Nicaragua, Iran was seeking political cooperation. By way of example, he floated the possibility of offering young Nicaraguan diplomats the opportunity to gain experience in Iran.

On August 1, 2007, only shortly after President Ortega's visit to Tehran, Iran sent its largest delegation yet to Nicaragua—or, at least, its largest *official* delegation. The group included 20 civil servants and businessmen who, during a six-day tour, studied ways in which political and commercial ties between the two nations could be strengthened.

These civil servants and businessmen represented the main areas of collaboration identified by Iran and Nicaragua over the preceding eight months: energy, technology for irrigation and potable water, agribusiness, and infrastructure. The trip was presented as an effort to turn the long list of promises of cooperation between Iran and Nicaragua into specifics. Thus, President Ortega announced that the Iranian government would be studying the possibility of constructing a US$ 350 million deepwater port on Nicaragua's Caribbean coast.[12] This was part of a package deal that included a promise from Iran to support Nicaraguan efforts to build power plants with 616 megawatts of capacity. The value of the total package was estimated at over US$ 1.2 billion. During the Iranian delegation's visit, representatives of the Ortega administration stated that they had proposed a portfolio of projects worth roughly US$ 1 billion.

In the area of agriculture, the Iranian delegation indicated that it would provide the country with 4,000 tractors, in addition to offering support for dairy plants, an industrial slaughterhouse, health clinics, and 10,000 low-income housing units over the next five years.[13] Then, on September 27, 2007, at the Annual General Meeting of the United Nations, the Iranian President offered to build a hospital in Nicaragua to provide care for victims of Hurricane Mitch. As of early July 2008, no information was available on whether plans for this hospital had proceeded.[14]

An Operational Question regarding the Construction of a Hydroelectric Plant

In early March of 2008, the Nicaraguan press reported new promises of collaboration between Managua and Tehran. On that occasion, the Iranian press agency announced that the Iranian Majles (parliament) had approved a loan of 150 million euros for the construction of a dam and electric power plant in Nicaragua's northern Caribbean region.[15] Terms of the agreement would require the Nicaraguan government to repay the loan over ten years, at 5 percent interest (for total interest of 11 million euros). In contrast to the other promises and agreements for Iranian-Nicaraguan cooperation made and signed during that twelve-month period, Nicaraguan officials and spokespersons avoided giving any details regarding the scope of the loan reportedly offered by the Iranian Parliament. As of the writing of this report, little, if anything, is known about this operation, which—if it were actually to occur—would have to be submitted to the Nicaraguan legislature for approval.

In the days after news broke regarding the Iranian loan for the construction of a hydroelectric dam, the opposition Sandinista Renovation Movement (Movimiento de Renovación Sandinista, or MRS) publicly denounced the loan as disadvantageous. Its main argument was that the interest rate for the loan was more than double the rate offered by other multilateral lending institutions, such as the Inter-American Development Bank and the World Bank. Moreover, the form in which the Nicaraguan government was to administer the loan aroused suspicion, since it afforded benefits to Ortega political operatives and provided for privatizing nearly all Venezuelan cooperation deriving from energy agreements between Venezuela and Nicaragua.[16]

An "Announced" Trip to Iran

Describing a meeting held on May 1, 2008, with the Iranian ambassador, in one of the customary and highly attended "People's President" events, Ortega announced that he had asked his Iranian counterpart to support and finance a program to help invigorate Nicaragua's agricultural sector.[17] The request that Ortega cited on that occasion was, in fact, nothing more than a reiteration of previous statements that the Iranian and Sandinista governments had been making for more than a year on cooperation involving milk processing plants, tractors, agribusiness technology, and hydroelectric dams and plants.

Then, in June of 2008, perhaps in a desperate attempt by the Government to "put the pedal to the metal" and make good on at least some of the many cooperative agreements between Nicaragua and Iran, President Ortega once again planned a trip to Tehran. No government representative at the time was able, or willing, to offer an explanation of the trip's objectives and, to date, the Government has made no official statement on whether such a trip ever did, in fact, take place—or, if so, its purpose. The trip had been planned to coincide with the World Food Summit convened by the Food and Agriculture Organization of the United Nations, which Ortega did not attend. Moving forward in time to when the present report is being written, little is known—publicly, at least—about the status of the Iranian-Nicaraguan economic, political, and trade cooperation process. Cooperation will certainly take place, although not on the scale that President Ortega has in mind. Within the President's closest circles, there is a growing sense that cooperation with Iran would represent the second great step towards accessing resources—a move that would free Ortega of the need to cooperate with the United States or Europe and, thus, of the commitments to transparency and accountability entailed in accepting funds—and the associated conditions—from those sources.

There is already a general sense in Nicaragua that cooperation with Iran is more theory than reality, and that the Iranian Government is taking advantage of the expectations it is generating among members of the Sandinista government, as Iran maneuvers to install a political and operational base in Nicaragua, while providing almost nothing in exchange.

Fundamental Doubts about Iranian-Nicaraguan Relations and Cooperation?

As early as the first days of January 2007, only weeks after Ortega assumed office, Nicaraguan analysts began, based on two factors, to doubt the viability of relations with Iran, and to question the intent to engage in any real cooperation. First, Nicaragua could face serious consequences for cooperating with a country that does not respect the authority of the United Nations and that is essentially anti-American, anti-Israeli, and generally anti-West. Second, economic and trade relations—and, in the 1980s, even political relations—between Nicaragua and Iran have been marginal at best.

Fears about the Iranian-Nicaraguan Relationship

The initial reactions to potential relations between Nicaragua and Iran began to emerge after Ahmadinejad's visit to Managua. Emilio Álvarez Montalbán, who was Minister of Foreign Affairs for the first two years of President Alemán's administration, suggested that Ahmadinejad's visit created an atmosphere of suspicion, uncertainty and fear, adding that the relationship between Nicaragua and the United States has been "clouded" by the long and well-documented tension between the U.S. and Iran.[18] The former Minister's opinions were also based on speeches Ortega made shortly after being elected, in which he unequivocally aligned himself—at least rhetorically—with an anti-U.S. Latin American bloc headed by Venezuelan President Hugo Chávez.

Indeed, the fear and suspicion that Nicaragua would shift its focus of interest from the United States towards an anti-American bloc led by Chávez, and supported by Iran, became a reality several months later, when President Ortega, at the United Nations General Assembly, stated his unconditional support for Iran's right to pursue uranium enrichment, directly opposing the position that the Security Council had adopted in March of 2007.

Domestic opponents of the Sandinista government, as well as some foreign policy experts in the United States, found their fears about Iranian-Nicaraguan relations even more roundly justified by Ortega's trip to Tehran in June of 2007.

Domestically, the Nicaraguan President's visit to Iran was seen as an initiative rather than as the closing of a deal—an act designed more to cater to Ortega's anti-American political base than to actually secure any specific trade benefit. According to academic and political analysts, this view of Ortega is based on the President's romantic and messianic self-identification as a world-class leader, committed to the most wide-ranging expressions of "anti-Americanism." Francisco Aguirre Sacasa, who formerly headed the Ministry of Foreign Affairs and who is one of the strongest links in the chain between Ortega and Alemán, invoked the phrase "politics of the heart," a term used by the Nicaraguan press to describe the Ortega-Iran relationship.[19] The phrase perhaps most aptly characterizes Nicaragua's *criollo* politics, and is duly suggestive of the implications of a governmental stance that takes great pains to reclaim, nurture and value relationships that support its anti-American ideology, while at the same time striving to maintain a more or less cordial relationship with its northern neighbor. This largely summarizes the state of U.S.-Nicaraguan relations during the first ten months of the Sandinista administration. "To me," says Aguirre Sacasa, "it seems that this country—that the Ortega government—has its heart in one hand and its head in the other... This policy has reached the point of schizophrenia." On one hand, Ortega maintains a "correct" relationship with the United States (as regards international finance), while on the other he "takes the bull by the horns" with his "virulent speeches." In an interview with the Nicaraguan weekly magazine *Confidencial*, Aguirre Sacasa adds that the United States response has seemed "sophisticated" in comparison to events of the past six years. "They allow Daniel Ortega to give controversial speeches as long as they don't jeopardize the United States's basic Central American agenda, namely, achieving democracy in the region—an agenda that mandates non-interference in the electoral processes of neighboring Guatemala and El Salvador, and combating drug trafficking and international crime."

This is, perhaps, one of the few explicit points of reference that can be found regarding the ideological inspiration for the Sandinista government's foreign policy, which has recently been explained as follows by historian, diplomat, and international affairs advisor to the governing party, Aldo Díaz Lacavo:

> "No country on Earth—absolutely none—can stick its head in the sand like an ostrich and deny that this world is a world in flux. Nobody can deny that this fluctuating world is being twisted by Northern countries, and in particular by the United States. The

world must react against this twisting caused by the North and the United States. This is an absolutely visible, tangible reality. The FSLN [Sandinista National Liberation Front] has a specific, well-defined interpretation of, and position on, this twisting, one that it believes provides the best possible path toward a better world. That is why it is unconcerned by the risks it is taking."

It was perhaps the reality of the risks involved in opposing the United States that brought Ortega himself to affirm that the Iranian and Nicaraguan revolutions—both of which occurred in 1979—were "twin revolutions, with the same objectives of justice, freedom, sovereignty and peace"—a reaction to "aggressive, imperialistic policies."[20] Then, in September of 2007, at the United Nations, he focused his speech on world problems, expressing resounding, almost solitary, support for Ahmadinejad.

Conclusion: From Words to Deeds

The following table[21] outlines the scope of the numerous agreements between Nicaragua and Iran. Not surprisingly, a great deal of information is missing—information that the Nicaraguan political machine, with an almost fervent determination (similar to that with which it guards records of its cooperation with Venezuela) keeps under lock and key. Indeed, evidence shows that the Ortega government's handling of ideological cooperation represents a nontransparent paradigm *par excellence.*

In conclusion, in terms of the reality of Iranian cooperation with Nicaragua, there is no indication that that it will be comparable, in the short term, to the aid provided to Nicaragua by the United States and the rest of the world. Indeed, since the beginning of 2008, Nicaraguan press reports have repeatedly pointed out that, after more than a year of trips, hugs, kisses and speeches, actual Iranian support for Nicaragua has been minimal, if not nonexistent.[22] Moreover, it would be hard to imagine Iranian aid becoming comparable to the medium- or long-range support provided by Venezuela, in terms of either total amount or degree of discretionality of the funds provided. Lastly, this cooperation

Current Status of Agreements Between Nicaragua and Iran, as of the date of the Technical Visit of the Iranian Delegation to Nicaragua on August 4, 2007

Energy and Mining Sector	Brito Hydroelectric Project (616 megawatts, at a cost of US$ 1.2 billion).	Project to generate power in the Estrella community. No public information available on total project cost.	Project to generate power in the Piedra Puntuda community. No public information available on total project cost.	Boboque Project (70 megawatts), funded by a 150-million euro loan, to be repaid over ten years. Total interest: 11 million euros.
Agriculture and Forestry Sector	Provision of 4,000 tractors of various sizes. No public information available on total project cost.	Construction of 5 milk processing plants and 10 milk collection centers. No public information available on total project cost.	Provision of modern equipment for irrigation system. No public information available on total project cost.	Training courses and workshops on agricultural development topics. No public information available on total project cost.
Health Sector	Installation of a medical clinic in Managua. No public information available on total project cost.	Training of health personnel. No public information available on total project cost.	Reconstruction of health centers and clinics. No public information available on total project cost.	Provision of high-tech laboratories. No public information available on total project cost.
Port Sector	Construction of two ports in Muelle de Corinto. Estimated investment: US$ 36 million.	Construction of a deep water port at Money Point. Estimated investment: US$ 350 million.		
Urban and Rural Housing Sector	Construction of 10,000 low-income housing units over the next 5 years. No public information available on total project cost.	Long-term mortgage loan to the domestic financial system. No public information available on total project cost.		
Water and Sanitation Sector	Short- and medium-term plans to drill 10 to 20 wells. No public information available on total project cost.	Improvement and rehabilitation of existing water distribution network. No public information available on total project cost.	Studies on supplying water from alternative sources. No public information available on total project cost.	

has changed the rules of the game in regard to transparency and public accountability.

NOTES

1 With his first campaign, in 1984, Ortega won 67 percent of the vote. Violeta de Chamorro was elected with 54.7 percent of votes in 1990, Arnoldo Alemán with 51 percent in 1996 and Enrique Bolaños with 56 percent in 2001.

2 The Democracy Index categorizes countries in terms of four types of regimes, based on their level of democratic development: (1) complete democracies; (2) imperfect democracies; (3) hybrid regimes; and (4) authoritarian regimes.

3 The data released by the IDD show only six countries as being above average—three (Chile, Costa Rica and Uruguay) with high levels of democratic development (above 7.51) and three others (Argentina, Mexico, and Panama) with scores greater than 5. The remaining 12 nations (El Salvador, Bolivia, Brazil, Colombia, Ecuador, Guatemala, Honduras, Nicaragua, Paraguay, Peru, the Dominican Republic, and Venezuela) all scored below 5.

4 Presentation by the development expert and consultant Diógenes Ruiz at the First IEEPP Forum on Transparency in the Administration of Cooperation for Development, held in Managua on April 2, 2008. See "La cooperación venezolana y los desafíos para la transparencia" (IEEPP, July 2008).

5 ECLAC preliminary figures estimate a 3 percent growth for 2008 and 19.6 percent inflation rate.

6 For example, in a little over two decades, Costa Rica managed to increase its energy production capacity some 235 percent, with Honduras registering a rise of 342 percent and Nicaragua only 139 percent. Nevertheless, in Costa Rica's case, the increase in energy generating capacity has nearly tripled for hydroelectric energy, with a mere 20 percent increase in thermal energy generation. In Honduras, hydroelectric energy increased by more than 150 percent, whereas thermal production increased by 14.5 percent. Finally, Nicaragua, unlike the other Central American countries that are increasing their production, saw the scant existing hydroelectric energy production drop by 60 percent, while thermal production nearly quadrupled.

7 http://impreso.elnuevodiario.com.ni/2007/01/14/nacionales/38792

8 On march 24th, the United Nations approved maintaining sanctions on Iran.

9 This resolution was unanimously approved by the United Nations Security Council at its 5647th meeting, on March 24th, 2007.

10 "Irán suspende cooperación con OIEA." El Nuevo Diario. March 25th, 2007. Ed. 9559. Managua, Nicaragua.

11 "Ortega de visita en Irán." http://news.bbc.co.uk/hi/spanish/latin_america/newsid_6739000/6739657.stm

12 "Ortega recibe misión Iraní." http://www.laprensa.com.ni/archivo/2007/agosto/01/noticias/ultimahora/206902.shtml

13 "Misión Iraní interesada en cuatro proyecto hidroeléctricos en Nicaragua." http://impreso.elnuevodiario.com.ni/2007/08/04/nacionales/55485

14 The real proof is that the only hospital with foreign funding operating after the hurricane was a field hospital donated by Cuba, and the doctors who worked there were Cuban doctors. There is also evidence that an Iranian delegation traveled to a number of locations in the Northern Caribbean region to assess damage from the hurricane. These visits did not result in any actual aid for the people inhabiting those areas.

15 "Irán ofrece préstamo a Nicaragua para construir central hidroeléctrica." http://www.elnuevodiario.com.ni/nacionales/10484

16 For more information on the characteristics and implications of Venezuelan cooperation with Nicaragua, see "La cooperación venezolana y los desafíos para la transparencia del sector público de Nicaragua." Institute for Strategic Studies and Public Policy. July 2008.

17 "Ortega pide a Irán fondos para sector agrícola."

18 "Tensión EE. UU. – Irán enturbia." El panorama. http://www.confidencial.com.ni/2007-518/politica2_518.html

19 "Política exterior y la gira presindencial." http://www.confidencial.com.ni/2007-538/politica_538.html

20 See: http://www.conamornicaragua.org.ni/documentos_4/junio/LA%20FORTALEZA%20DE%20LOS%20PUEBLOS%20Palabras%20DOS%20en%20Univ%20Teheran%20100607.doc

21 For the full, detailed report, see: http://www.conamornicaragua.org.ni/documentos_4/agosto/DECLARACION%20CONJUNTA%20NICARAGUA_IRAN.doc.

22 "Ya pasó un año y nada con Irán." http://blogs.elnuevodiario.com.ni/2008/01/21/nacionales/68399

BOLIVIAN FOREIGN POLICY: Observations on the Bolivia-Iran Relationship

GUSTAVO FERNÁNDEZ

EXTERNAL IMAGE

The current foreign policy of the Evo Morales government is built around two images. The first is that of an historical indigenous-claims movement, intended to put a full stop after five hundred years of ethnic exploitation and marginalization (a thesis, however, that ignores the historical significance of the revolution of 1952). At the center of the image is the figure of the President, an indigenous union leader propelled into power on the shoulders—and votes—of the people. His popular base is the coca growers' unions and the social movements of the *altiplano*, inspired by a group of Aymara intellectuals. The simple (and deceptive) cliché of an Indian President for an Indian country was well received in the international community. It mattered not what the President would do; it sufficed that he was there. This, at least, seemed to be the judgment of international observers, and was the logic behind nominating the President of Bolivia for a Nobel Prize—casting him, in the wake of Rigoberta Menchú, as an Andean Mandela.

It was predictable that such a campaign would attempt to make Morales the leader of the entire continent's indigenous peoples, particularly those of Peru, Ecuador, Guatemala and Mexico. But when the image ceased to be merely symbolic, and assumed more tangible political connotations, the governments of those countries, as well as the peasant movements themselves, rejected this intrusion into their domestic politics.

The second image, which has gradually been replacing the first, is that of a revolutionary, anti-imperialist movement determined to construct the socialism of the twenty-first century. The nationalization of the oil and telecommunications companies and the expulsion of the U.S. ambassador fit this second image better than it did the first. The core political group that actually runs the government—composed of the remnants of the country's leftist parties—is repeating the nationalist motifs of the seventies. Along with Venezuela, Cuba and Nicaragua, it proposes to construct a type of Latin American socialist camp, a regional version of the market socialism or authoritarian capitalism pursued by China and Vietnam, with the difference that those countries seek to bring their economies fully into the mainstream of globalized trade and production, while their regional imitators reject any such attempt.

The agents of Bolivia's foreign policy seem to see no conflict in advocating the principles of self-determination and nationalism while at the same time proclaiming their belief in socialist internationalism—two concepts that logic and practice have shown to be in opposition. The government claims national independence and sovereignty as the basis of its foreign policy, but does not hesitate to issue opinions on the domestic politics of other states, or to allow other countries to intervene in its own domestic politics, as occurred with Venezuela, which has established a sort of de facto tutelage over governmental behavior and events in Bolivia.

Domestically, the Aymara movement's attempt to constitutionally impose the hegemony of its culture, its plans for State control of the economy, the centralization of power, and the neutralizing of democratic institutions—moves endorsed by the political wing of the government—has encountered resistance, first in the country's eastern departments and then in the valley cities, under the rallying cry of autonomy.

External context

Morales came into power on the continental wave that rejected the open market economy model, foreign investment and transnational corporations. Political systems were renewed throughout the region, governing elites were replaced, and the predominance of politics over technocracy—and of the State over the market—was restored. The nature of the region's insertion in the global system had to be altered, but without severing its links to the dynamic nuclei of trade and the production of goods and knowledge.

The Bolivian government, too, pursued these objectives, but precipitously, and without regard for the optics. The photograph showing the oil fields occupied by military forces was seen around the world, and evoked the clumsy, strong-armed confiscations of totalitarian regimes, rather than the image of a democratic society exercising the right to control its own resources.

The Morales government did benefit from the expansion of the country's productive frontier—the consequence of twenty years of democracy—as well as from the rising price of raw materials on the world market. Together, these factors increased the country's export potential fivefold, giving the State an extraordinary degree of economic and political autonomy. Thus, without lifting a finger, the Movement for Socialism (known by its Spanish acronym MAS) found itself freed from financial dependence on cooperation funds or on the conditionalities associated with international organizations, and from the constraints confronted by the governments that built Bolivian democracy—beginning with the People's Democratic Unity Party (Unidad Democrática y Popular) of President Siles Zuazo.

Allies and enemies

Evo Morales's foreign policy is based on a strategic alliance with Venezuela and Cuba. Bolivian dependence is no longer financial —Bolivia was once financially dependent on the United States and the IMF—. The balancing of the Bolivian budget does not require donations from Venezuela, and the country's exports do not depend on access to the Cuban or Venezuelan market (in contrast to Nicaragua and Cuba, which could not balance their energy equations without Venezuelan support). ALBA (the Spanish acronym for the Bolivarian Alternative for the Americas) is a mere acronym, with no trade implications or practical significance. Donations to Bolivia by its Caribbean neighbor, which total some seventy million dollars, are strictly marginal—in an economy that now has more than six billion dollars of currency reserves. However, these funds can be used discretionally, without controls, for propaganda campaigns or to finance secret expenditures or security operations. PDVSA's investment in oil exploration went unannounced, and only recently, with the purchases of PRODEM and Gravetal, has the presence of Venezuelan capital in the Bolivian economy been evident.

The explanation for this dependency relationship appears to be political and personal, since even in terms of historical perspective Morales is at odds with the views espoused by Comandante Chávez. Thus, the indigenous movement of Evo Morales rejects the Republic that Simón Bolívar liberated, as being a *criollo* extension of the regime that exploited the continent's original peoples—one that cannot, therefore, be "Bolivarian."

The tactical agreements with Ecuador and the "alliances" with Nicaragua and Iran are of a different nature. Correa's own view of revolutionary change in Ecuador is similar—but not subordinate—to the Bolivarian project, with latitude to agree or disagree on a case-by-case basis.[1] Ortega has closer links with Venezuela, but from Bolivia's perspective, Ortega is not Fidel Castro, nor does he possess the sort of resources that Hugo Chávez can offer. Iran will be discussed a bit further on.

What really unites these regimes is their rejection of the policies of George W. Bush and of the United States, which they term imperial—with particularly radical connotations in the cases of Chávez, Ortega and Morales. For various reasons, Brazil, Argentina, Chile, Ecuador and Mexico also have serious disagreements with the United States administration and its foreign policy, particularly on Iraq, but they manage those disagreements as pragmatic matters—as differences of State—not as personal or ideological ones, as do the leaders of ALBA.

One might even say that Morales has gone further than Chávez and Ortega in his rejection of United States policy. Indeed, after repeatedly denouncing intervention in domestic politics by diplomatic agents, he concluded by declaring the United States ambassador persona non grata, and asked the DEA and USAID to leave the country. He supported a march organized by social movements, which ended up at the doors of the U.S. Embassy, and fired the head of the police, who prevented the marchers from taking over the building.

Ambassador Goldberg returned to Washington, and the United States government responded with a rapid series of actions showing that it had decided to abandon the cautious line previously taken by the State Department. Not surprisingly, the U.S. declared the Bolivian ambassador persona non grata, then, in a more concrete step, removed Bolivia from the list of countries actively combating drug trafficking. As a result of this de-listing, Bolivia was not included in the request for expanded trade benefits under the Andean Trade Promotion and Drug Eradication Act. This endangered the jobs of 15,000 direct employees and approximately 35,000 indirect employees at light-manufacturing export firms in the urban centers of El Alto and Cochabamba.

The European countries have not yet decided how to react to the Bolivian government's acts of aggression against firms like Repsol and ENTEL. They felt certain that the anti-imperialist salvos would not be pointed in their direction, that Morales would recognize the support that European NGOs and governments were providing. They now feel that the Bolivian President failed to honor the explicit commitment he made in various meetings with European heads of government during his first international tour. They are increasingly disturbed by his unnecessary—and, from any perspective, provocative—rapprochement with Iran. Things have now reached the point where European support is no longer the unqualified support it used to be—support that may, in fact, turn into open opposition should matters continue on their current course. In an unusual move, the European Commission suspended its fourth round of negotiations with the Andean Community, principally because of the Bolivian position, which makes an Andean consensus impossible.

The neighborhood

Bolivia has had well-established economic, financial and technological links with the industrial powers, Europe and the United States. These served as export destinations for Bolivia's silver, tin, rubber and coca paste, while being the source of Bolivia's inflows of investment, technology and manufactured goods.

This relationship has changed. South America has become, for the first time in Bolivia's history, the country's primary route to participation in the global economy.

The neighborhood has always been the testing ground for Bolivia's geopolitical and political relationships. It was with bordering countries that it waged its wars, and it was from those countries that threats to Bolivia's existence as a State emanated. Its politicians forged friendships and alliances with their colleagues in neighboring countries, and took refuge in—or were exiled to—them. As we have seen, the moment

Morales chose Venezuela and Cuba as the guiding star of his foreign policy, the historical axis of those regional political alliances shifted—at least for the moment.

In reality, the country's commercial and economic links—which ultimately will determine the true direction of its political affiliations—continue to be firmly anchored in Brazil, Argentina, Chile, Peru and Colombia and, in terms of light manufacturing, in the United States. Natural gas, soy, tropical crops, labor-intensive manufactured goods, tourism and services are the weft on which the design of Bolivia's economic life will be woven in the twenty-first century. They constitute the true stage for Bolivia's geopolitical life, as well as its economic field of action, and this entrenched reality does not allow for media or propaganda manipulations. That is what Brazilian President Luiz Inácio Lula da Silva tried to communicate to Morales when he pointed to Venezuela on a map, and then to Brazil, with its more than three thousand kilometers of border with Bolivia.

In May of 2006, Morales nationalized the oil industry and ordered the armed forces to occupy the Petrobrás oil fields and refineries. This move, perhaps more than the political decision itself—which recalled the period of the military governments, when the Bolivian Left denounced what was then known as Brazilian "sub-imperialism"—deeply offended Brazil's government and public, which judged it to be unnecessarily aggressive and unfriendly. The government's first reaction was to suspend its investment in the petroleum sector and all plans for bilateral cooperation. Later, it normalized relations, but the relationship has never returned to its previous status. Petrobrás proceeded with investments essential to produce enough gas to meet its own demand, but declined a request to make some of the volume available to Argentina, and refused to invest in developing fields to produce natural gas for Argentina. Lula avoided direct confrontation, despite pressure from Brazil's business/diplomatic/military establishment, which demanded a firmer response. Nevertheless, delays began to be seen in cooperation programs involving petrochemicals, infrastructure, agriculture and industrial development that had been announced in the initial months of the Morales government. The relationship between the two countries is now reasonably cordial, but its initial closeness is gone.

Argentina agreed to renegotiate the price of the natural gas it bought from Bolivia, thus contributing to the initial success of the Morales government's measures. Beyond the fact that there is a certain ideological convergence between the Kirchner government and the Bolivian government, this gesture was a clear sign of Buenos Aires's interest in establishing a strategic relationship with Bolivia, re-establishing the former relationship that was scuttled when it shifted its sights to Brazil in the early 1990s and stopped buying Bolivian natural gas. Later, in 2007, Bolivia signed an agreement to sell Argentina 27.7 million cubic meters per day of natural gas in 2010—an arrangement similar to that reached with Brazil. In turn, the purchaser assumed the obligation of building the northeastern pipeline that would bring the gas to its centers of consumption. The government of Néstor and Cristina Kirchner needs the natural gas and made a major political investment in that contract. It was therefore highly displeased when it became clear that the Morales government did not have the production volumes it had promised to deliver, and that this situation would not change during Morales's term. Like Brazil, however, Argentina decided it would gain little by demanding that Bolivia pay the contractual non-performance penalties. And while it did not break ties with Morales, it did begin to maintain its distance.

Surprisingly, relations with Chile are more friendly and cordial, although yielding a similar lack of concrete results. Little progress has been made in providing Bolivian natural gas to the Chilean market, for the simple reason that investment, reserves and production have declined since the nationalization of May 2006. A more than twenty year negotiation has just concluded, providing equal treatment for Bolivian freight in Iquique to that given in Arica, but there is no sign of progress on the Bolivian demand for sovereign access to the Pacific through territory in Chile's possession. Chile's Presidential Palace has been noticeably content with the status quo—explainable by the fact that its ongoing dialogue with Morales has diluted any diplomatic action by Bolivia in multilateral fora and neutralized any other initiatives, which, if taken, might have aggravated the crisis posed by Peru's demand to delimit the maritime border between Peru and Chile.

At the same time, there are numerous signs of tension in the bilateral relationship between Peru and Bolivia. Morales openly supported the candidacy of Ollanta Humala in the election that was ultimately won by Alan García, and the Lima press has repeatedly denounced Morales's alleged influence on the indigenous and coca growers' movements in the mountains of southern Peru. The conflict was ratcheted up when Bolivia opposed Peru's request that the Andean Community modify its intellectual property rules—an absolute prerequisite to Peru's signing a free trade agreement with the United States. Peru, in turn, vetoed Bolivia's candidate for the UNASUR Secretariat, and on June 30, the Peruvian government recalled its ambassador in La Paz for consultation to protest statements by President Morales urging the Peruvian people to resist any establishment of American military bases on its territory. This altercation culminated in an exchange of verbal hostilities between the presidents of the two countries.

Thus it would appear that Bolivia's relations with its neighbors are not particularly close or productive. In the case of Brazil and Argentina, they turned from openly friendly to politically correct; relations with Chile serve the functional needs of trans-Andean Bolivia; while the relationship with Peru is openly hostile. It is still too early to gauge Morales's relations with President Lugo of Paraguay.

One further point is worth noting. The resounding victory of the opposition in four autonomy referenda in departments bordering Brazil and Argentina, where the natural gas fields and soy farms are located—to say nothing of the recent election of a new opposition Prefect in Chuquisaca—will sooner or later be the object of strategic assessment in those countries, which, among other things, based their support for Morales on confidence that he would engage in a long-term dialogue.

THE BILATERAL RELATIONSHIP WITH IRAN

The framework agreement

On September 27, 2007, President Ahmadinejad made a several-hour visit to La Paz, arriving before noon and leaving at three in the afternoon for Caracas where he and President Evo Morales met and signed a joint declaration and framework agreement, and their ministers signed memoranda of understanding. Ahmadinejad summarized his view of the meeting saying, "The people of Iran and the Bolivian people have decided to join hands to build their countries. They have decided to be mutual comrades in difficult situations, and to share their pains and joys."

In the joint declaration, which establishes a $1.1 billion industrial cooperation plan for the 2007-2012 period, the two presidents stressed their countries' right to develop nuclear energy for peaceful purposes in the framework of the Nuclear Non-Proliferation Treaty, as a significant step towards meeting their peoples' needs for economic and technological development, and reiterated their commitment to support political actions to promote the development of a multi-polar world, in order to ensure greater balance and democratization in international relations.

The declaratory portion of the framework agreement refers to:

- A commitment to multilateralism within a framework of full respect for the rules and principles of international law and of the United Nations Charter—in particular, to the principles of the sovereign equality of States, the prohibition of threats or force against the territorial integrity or political independence of any State, self-determination, non-intervention in the internal affairs of States, and recognition of the right of peoples to develop and choose their economic and sociopolitical development model.

- Working to consolidate the positive changes and trends manifest in the world with the emergence of political regimes opposed to neoliberalism—regimes that promote social policies and genuine integration and cooperation, while defending the national interests of their peoples against hegemonic purposes.

- Strengthening political dialogue in order to deepen and diversify diplomatic relations between the two countries and establish common bases for the signing of future bilateral documents.

The principal objective of the agreement is to take advantage of energy resources for the benefit of the two states. Under the framework agreement the cooperation will focus on hydrocarbons, mining, production, industry, agriculture, infrastructure, water, forestry, culture, science and technology, management of natural resources, construction and manufacturing. To this end, funding of one hundred million dollars is contemplated to facilitate execution of the agreements (with the use of the funds to be regulated), along with a five-year billion-dollar industrial cooperation plan to be administered by a Binational Technical Commission, designed to expand bilateral cooperation and ensure its long-term continuity.

The sectoral ministries of the two countries will establish binational technical committees to develop and implement sectoral agreements, cooperation programs and projects and in their areas of authority. The ministries of foreign affairs will supervise and evaluate compliance with the framework agreement, sectoral agreements and other bilateral instruments, through a joint commission that will meet periodically. At the same time, on the purely political front, the ministries of foreign affairs, through an exchange of letters, will establish a political consultation mechanism involving periodic meetings to analyze all aspects of the countries' bilateral relations and to exchange views on international matters of mutual interest.

Memoranda of Understanding

In addition, the following memoranda of understanding were signed:

(a) Memorandum of understanding on agricultural mechanization and modernization, and on rural development, signed by Susan Rivero and her Iranian counterpart.

The purpose of this MOA is to foster research on technological development in agriculture, livestock and forestry, and to promote exchanges in science and technology, with an emphasis on rational and sustainable use of natural resources. Its objective is to establish an institutional framework that facilitates technical and scientific cooperation through the joint design and execution of programs and projects in agriculture, natural resource management, agricultural mechanization and modernization, and rural development. The countries express their mutual interest in carrying out cooperative research on plants, seeds, forests, grasses, livestock, fish farming, genetic research on soil and water, and cooperative activities involving agricultural machinery and the forest industry. The memorandum also refers to mechanization in livestock raising, treatment for diseases of agricultural plants, animal diseases and other veterinary issues, livestock vaccines, apiculture, and wood resources.

(b) Memorandum of understanding to develop trade, cooperation and technical assistance between the two countries, signed by Celina Sosa, Bolivia's Minister of Production and Micro-Enterprise, and Iran's Vice-Minister of Industry, Mohsen Shaterzadeh.

The MOA provides for the creation of a binational technical committee to undertake initiatives for trade development, cooperation and technical assistance between the two countries. Its objective is to carry out technology transfer, foster strategic industries and promote trade, as well as to implement business management programs. The two countries express their desire to work toward, initiate and develop cooperation activities of an economic, commercial, cultural, scientific, technological, investment, construction and manufacturing nature, and other such activities to be agreed upon at a later time.

(c) Memorandum of understanding to strengthen joint cooperation and energy complementarity, signed by Carlos Villegas, Bolivian Minister of Hydrocarbons, and Iran's Vice-Minister of Petroleum, H. Noghrehkar Shirazi.

The objective of the MOA is to facilitate technology transfer and training, and to provide for investment in hydrocarbons and electricity, by creating joint-venture enterprises, or any other applicable contractual form, with the participation of State enterprises. YPFB and the Iranian Oil Company will form joint-venture enterprises for drilling in Bolivia and for exploration and production of hydrocarbon reserves, as well as to establish petrochemical plants for the production of natural gas.

Television station

On February 19 of this year, President Evo Morales announced that the Government of the Islamic Republic of Iran was interested in installing a television station in the Cochabamba/Chapare region from which to broadcast its Latin American signal. "Iran has offered to install a television station in the Chapare region for all of Bolivia, for all of Latin America," proclaimed the President at the closing of the Eleventh Congress of the six federations of coca leaf farmers of the Tropic of Cochabamba.

The President stated that this was in recognition of the struggles of the Tropic of Cochabamba peasant movement, which was responsible for putting him in office. He emphasized the Chapare region's role in the struggles of the peasant movement, and recalled the visit to the Cochabamba Valley by Venezuelan president Hugo Chávez, who referred to it as "the epicenter of the democratic revolution, the peasant movement."

When the President delivered his address to the National Congress, he stated that the first Iranian ambassador would soon present his credentials, thus formalizing diplomatic relations with that Islamic Republic.

Final Observations

There are many reasons to consider the Bolivia-Iran relationship an anomaly, i.e., a strange departure from normal Bolivian foreign policy. It has neither historical precedent nor a trade or economic rationale. It is difficult to find points in common between a radical indigenous government of Marxist origin and an Islamic theocracy. The possibility of generating trade between two nations separated by such enormous distances, in the absence of means of transportation and communications, is virtually nil. Nor is it clear how a system of technical cooperation could be established between cultures, languages and productive systems as different as those of these two countries. Even with regard to oil, it would be more rational to seek support from Petrobrás or PDVSA than from an Iranian company. Moreover, there are no signs (no signs have been detected, at least) that any of the agreements has been put into operation, and they will most likely remain in that inactive state.

However, that is not the crucial point. The framework agreement and memoranda of understanding are simply political acts, manifestations of a political affinity. They express the two governments' agreement on anti-imperialist policy aimed at the United States, a point underscored by Evo Morales's trip to Tehran in September of last year. Thus, it would be meaningless to analyze the recently established ties between Bolivia and Iran from the perspective of their economic or technical advantages and disadvantages, or in terms of the extent to which the agreements are being implemented and the commitments met. The relationship is a political act, and its consequences will not be economic, commercial or financial but rather, political.

In examining the Bolivia-Iran relationship, it would be wise to devote greater attention to its geopolitical implications on two different planes—one regional, the other (more recent) global. In economic and political terms, there are two distinct game plans in the region. One is that being pursued in South America by Peru, Colombia and Chile (and probably Uruguay), which seeks full participation in the global system through international trade agreements with the United States, the European Union and APEC. This plan is already well underway.

The other is led by Venezuela, and includes Bolivia, Nicaragua and, to a lesser extent, Ecuador. It seeks an older style of regional integration, with more demanding, if not outright restrictive, treatment of foreign investment, and looks askance at insertion in the world economy, with constant denunciations of the role of transnational companies.

In addition to these two main camps, with their different strategic visions, there is Brazil, which occupies a special position. Latin America no longer plays a major role in its development strategy, even with regard to energy. The discovery of the Tupí fields has made Brazil energy self-sufficient, giving it a degree of influence it never had. This new, and perhaps most important, element in the equation means that Brazil's energy security no longer depends on a strategic partnership with Venezuela or on natural gas from Bolivia.

Meanwhile, Argentina is once again experiencing domestic political problems, and its power in South America is clearly limited. The global financial crisis compels it to seek a long-term structural solution that does not rely on Venezuelan cooperation.

At the meeting of UNASUR presidents in Santiago, Chile, on September 15, 2008 to discuss the Bolivian crisis, these positions were sharply differentiated. Brazil and Chile, supported by Colombia, Argentina, Uruguay and Paraguay, held that a solution to Bolivia's internal conflicts must be found through dialogue, and without external intervention, maintaining respect for democratic institutions, territorial integrity and human rights. As far as is known, that position contrasted with the positions of Venezuela and Ecuador, which were seeking more active support for Morales.

Until very recently, these Latin American political processes could be seen as distinct political phenomena, distant from the routes and problems of global conflict. They were part of a regional power game, throughout the continent, in search of a new equilibrium that would reflect the differing degrees of influence of the various actors. As such they had little effect on relations with the United States, which, since it understood that its national security was not threatened, saw the region's political evolution through a somewhat distant lens.

Something new, however, has transpired, representing a qualitative change in the process and touching upon a new area of global confrontation with important strategic (security) implications. This new element is Venezuela's rapprochement with Russia. For some time now, there have been signs at the global level of a developing political camp opposed to the liberal democratic bloc. Unlike the twentieth-century confrontation between capitalism and socialism, the key to the conflict in this case is not a debate on the market economy and forms of ownership, but centers rather on the control of energy and other natural resources and, pointedly, on forms of government. Far from accepting the formulas for liberal democracy in the West (and in Japan and India), Russia and some of the other countries of the former Soviet Union have returned to the vertical exercise of power. China, for example, has maintained a single-party socialist regime. Thus, a combination of market economy and single-party government with centralized powers has emerged in a number of countries that previously were part of the socialist camp, spawning a model that some term "authoritarian capitalism," while others prefer to reprise the expression "state capitalism." China prefers the term "market socialism." At the same time, Middle-East oil producing countries, such as Iran, have their own theocratic forms of capitalist authoritarianism. As noted here, a number of Latin American governments share similarities with this pattern of behavior.

Russia's military action in Osetia and Abkhazia, and the subsequent diplomatic recognition of those States, redraws the geopolitical zones of influence, attempts to project national interests, and raises economic and political differences to the level of security concerns. This decision by Russia—which occurred with the United States weakened by the wars in Iraq and Afghanistan, as well as by a severe financial crisis—resulted from the country's conviction that its national security was being seriously threatened by the West, by the incorporation of Poland, Hungary, the Czech Republic and the Baltic States in NATO, by the revolutions in Ukraine and Georgia, and by the separation of Kosovo from Serbia. The decision to install anti-missile radars in Poland confirmed Russia's fears.

Although it is no longer the superpower it was during the last century, Russia is anxious to recover a respectable and major role in the international community commensurate with its status as a nuclear power and, with oil prices riding high, regain its economic strength. Today's Russia is not the Russia of 1990, with an economy in ruins, a demoralized army and a paralyzed government.

Russia began by undertaking actions on its immediate border, in its old sphere of influence. However, it is capable of going further, with serious implications for Western interests in Iran and Syria. Through the Caribbean, it holds the prospect of approaching the very doorstep of the United States. It is this process that explains Russia's increasing geopolitical rapprochement with Venezuela, Bolivia and Nicaragua (Ecuador remains a question).

Venezuela's purchases of airplanes, helicopters and rifles for nearly four billion dollars—and, more importantly, the visit by strategic Russian Blackjack bombers to Maiquetía last September 10th, and the announcement of joint maneuvers of Russia's northern fleet and Venezuela's navy next November—confirm the perception and cause concern within some governments.

Of course, this scenario—if indeed it plays out—is in no sense comparable to the nuclear balance of terror that characterized the twentieth century. Russia has regained strength, but it is not the Soviet Union. The socialist camp no longer exists, and Germany and central Europe are firmly aligned with the West. China, India and Asia have their own designs for power in the economic realm, and are not about to jeopardize this by associating themselves with the plans of the Russian Federation. China made this clear after the Osetia conflict, when it confined itself to reiterating its pragmatic stance of nurturing positive trade relations with the West, while expressing its displeasure at separatism and at meddling in the domestic affairs of other nations. On September 25, 2008, in the wake of agreements with Venezuela, a Chinese Foreign Ministry spokesman denied that military issues had been addressed during President Chávez's visit to Beijing.

The United States reaction was sarcastic. The Secretary of State described the delivery of "a few old Blackjack bombers to one of the few Latin American autocracies" as an anachronistic display of military power. In Brazil, on September 20, 2008, the newspaper *O Estado de São Paulo* published information leaked to it by the government expressing irritation at the growing military and diplomatic relations between Venezuela and Russia, with the possibility of an extension to Bolivia—a prospect that, according to the article, was already known to Itamaraty, the seat of Brazil's Ministry of Foreign Affairs. In the judgment of the Brazilian government, Venezuela is needlessly importing to Latin America a dispute between Russia and the United States, again making the region a pawn in the geopolitical chess game that should have ended with the fall of the Soviet Union.

The relationship between Brazil and Venezuela has been marked by sharp differences, but Itamaraty has managed them without resorting to the open confrontation advocated by the media, business and certain political circles. A few days after revealing its irritation concerning the Venezuelan-Russian agreements and the threats of military intervention in Bolivia, Itamaraty announced that there would be a meeting in Manaos between Chávez, Morales and Correa on September 30th.

Bolivia's rapprochement with Iran, which could initially be viewed as token and symbolic, can now be seen in a different light. This move was, from the outset, difficult to execute. It ran into opposition from the Jewish lobby in the United States and Latin America—particularly in Brazil, where it has a strong presence, and in Argentina, where there were two terrorist attacks which, according to the judges hearing the cases, were the work of Iran. It represented a rhetorical challenge to the United States and the European Union, but little more.

Now, however, it is provoking other concerns, touching on sensitive national security issues in both the United States and Brazil. Neither of these powers likes the idea of an extra-regional power like Russia placing its footprint in the center of the continent. Still, one must not be lured into sensationalism. None of these possibilities has made it off the drawing board or, as yet, become a reality. Nevertheless, they have triggered red lights and must be taken into account in any future analysis of Latin American and Bolivian geopolitics.

Notes

1 The relationship between the Morales and Correa governments does not appear to be very harmonious. Bolivia requested the removal of the Andean Community's Executive Secretary, who was Ecuadorian, and Ecuador opposed Bolivia's candidacy for the UNASUR Secretariat.

RECENT DIPLOMATIC DEVELOPMENTS BETWEEN ECUADOR AND IRAN: A Gesture of Sovereign Affirmation or Lukewarm Geopolitical Alignment?

CÉSAR MONTÚFAR[1]

In a surprising move in January 2007, Iranian President Mahmoud Ahmadinejad visited Ecuador to participate in the induction ceremony of his Ecuadorian counterpart, Rafael Correa. Since then, reciprocal trade agreements have been established between the two countries, and both governments have opened diplomatic offices in their respective capital cities. This incipient relationship between Ecuador and Iran should not be seen as an isolated incident, but rather as evidence of ongoing, cooperative developments taking place between Iran and other Latin American countries, including Venezuela, Bolivia, and Nicaragua.

The recent diplomatic relationship between Ecuador and Iran—unprecedented in the bilateral relations of both countries—has generated concerns about its geopolitical ramifications in both Europe and the United States. Javier Solana, the European Union's High Representative for the Common Foreign and Security Policy, argued that Ecuador's diplomatic approach would, along with Bolivia, Nicaragua, and Venezuela, be contributing to a "Latin American chorus" supportive of Tehran.[2] On the other hand, the United States Assistant Secretary of State for Western Hemisphere Affairs, Thomas Shannon, interpreted Ahmadinejad's tour in the region as proof that Iran is trying to use Latin America to intensify diplomatic pressure on Washington. "In Latin America, Iran sees a way to demonstrate that they can exert themselves on an international level... It's a way to push back on us," he said. "And we remind them about the continuing relationships that exist in the region between groups in Latin America and groups that we consider to be terrorist in the Middle East, especially Hezbollah and Hamas."[3]

But besides this warning, what is in play and what implications will the present diplomatic and trade relations between Ecuador and Iran have? Was there anything more than a simple diplomatic gesture involved in the appearance of the Iranian president at the Ecuadorian president's inauguration? Or will Ecuador become geopolitically aligned with Iran's foreign policy as Venezuela, Bolivia, and Nicaragua have? This short essay will attempt to answer these questions. To that end, we will first offer a brief examination of past diplomatic and commercial relationships between Ecuador and Iran. Next, we will analyze the positions taken by several different actors leading up to Ahmadinejad's visit to Ecuador and the implications of this visit; then, we review the events that have taken place up until the present day and what steps both nations have taken to realize this relationship; and finally, we conclude with an analysis on how to move forward, offering an interpretation of why Ecuador extended diplomatic relations with Iran, despite the risk of alienating trade and political partners like Argentina, the United States, and the European Union.

Diplomatic and Trade Antecedents to Ecuador-Iran Relations

Ecuador has had very little past trade or political contact with Iran. Except for sporadic interactions as part of OPEC (excluding the years 1992-2007 when Ecuador withdrew), which both nations have been members of since its inception, there has not been any direct bilateral relations between the two countries. In fact, trade and political representatives have never been sent to the other country's capital; the Iranian Embassy in Bogotá handles Iranian citizens in Ecuador, and the Ecuadorian Embassy in Egypt does the same for its citizens in Iran.

In the Ministry of Foreign Relations archives in Ecuador, the only document about Ecuadorian-Iranian relations before January 2007 is a joint declaration between both countries signed in May 1989, when the Islamic Republic of Iran's Minister of Petroleum visited Ecuador. This document refers to an agreement regarding the exchange of technical delegations in order to collaborate on oil and energy issues, such as exploration, production, transportation, refinement, and commercialization. This declaration also mentions the creation of a group of experts in Iran's agriculture and industrial sectors who would subsequently visit Ecuador in order to exchange information related to these industries.

Finally, this joint document affirms the intent to increase cooperation between Ecuador and Iran in other economic areas, and to promote a greater understanding of the people of both nations.[4] There are no additional references with respect to these issues agreed upon in this declaration, which leads us to theorize that they were never intended to be a part of this document, or that they were removed at some point during the deliberations.

In regards to trade between Ecuador and Iran, there has been minimal trade between Ecuador and Iran until recently. After the declaration of diplomatic relations in January 2007, the Corporation for Promotion of Exports and Imports (CORPEI), released a study on the possibilities of Ecuadorian-Iranian trade, as well as an evaluation of bilateral trade between 2000 and 2007. This study marks 2003 as a record year, with some USD $2.5 million in Ecuadorian exports to the Islamic nation. During that seven year period, the study demonstrates that Ecuador enjoyed a favorable trade balance with Iran in 2003, 2004, and 2005; during the other years, trade was more favorable to Iran.

EVOLUTION OF ECUADOR-IRAN TRADE

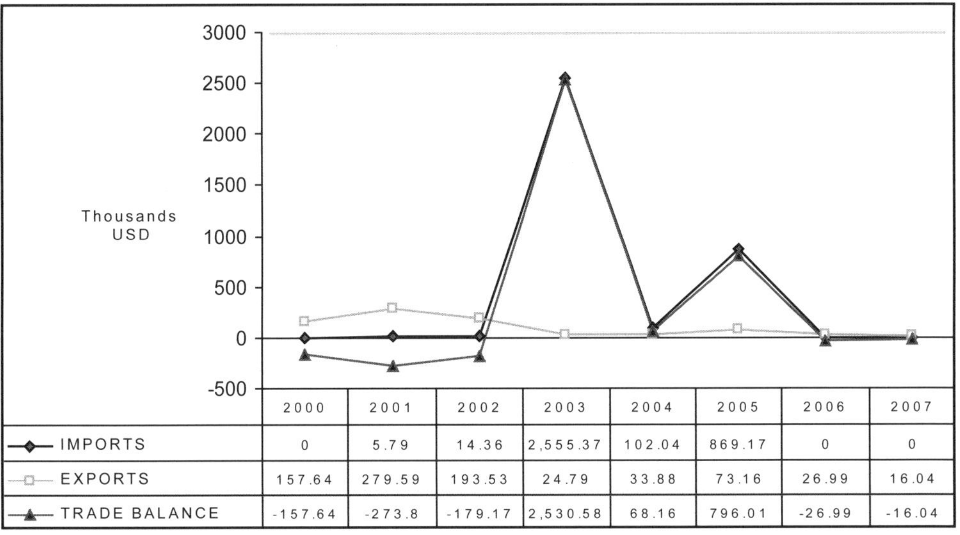

	2000	2001	2002	2003	2004	2005	2006	2007
IMPORTS	0	5.79	14.36	2,555.37	102.04	869.17	0	0
EXPORTS	157.64	279.59	193.53	24.79	33.88	73.16	26.99	16.04
TRADE BALANCE	-157.64	-273.8	-179.17	2,530.58	68.16	796.01	-26.99	-16.04

Source: Banco Central

Ecuador's surplus during that three-year span was due primarily to exports of coffee, bananas, and other fruits. Other products exported to Iran included flowers and palm oil. In 2000, 2006, and 2007, there were no Ecuadorian exports to Iran, which shows a sporadic, intermittent trade relationship and lack of a substantial, permanent economic partnership. Iranian imports by Ecuador consist mainly of luxury items such as dish sets, Persian rugs, spices, ceramic statuettes, bed linens, and car parts. In 2001, there was a relatively important shipment of tractors valued at some USD $141 thousand.[5]

The Surprising, Short, and Controversial Ahmadinejad Visit to Ecuador and its Implications

It was in this context of an all but nonexistent diplomatic and trade relationship (public or private) that, on January 15th, 2007, during the inaugural ceremonies for President Rafael Correa, Ecuador received a surprising, short, and controversial visit from the President of Iran, Mahmoud Ahmadinejad. He was in the country for only a couple of hours, but during that time, besides attending Correa's inauguration, he met personally with the newly-elected president, invited him to visit Iran, and offered him "any type of support, which could include investment agreements similar to those set up with Venezuela and Nicaragua, which could alleviate in part the debilitated Ecuadorian economy."[6] Ahmadinejad also took advantage of his brief stay in Quito to meet with Bolivian President Evo Morales, and it's worth remembering that his lightning-like visit to Ecuador was part of a broader tour of Latin America, including Nicaragua and Venezuela.

The Iranian President's visit to Ecuador was announced only a couple of days beforehand; nevertheless, it aroused strong questions domestically and especially internationally. Besides Javier Solana and Thomas Shannon, the most serious reaction came from Argentine President Néstor Kirchner, who—despite his close political relationship with Correa—refused to be present at the commencement ceremonies once Ahmadinejad's attendance was made public. However, Kirchner's refusal to attend Correa's inauguration did not affect the relationship between Argentina and Ecuador, one of the strongest relationships in

South America.[7] This is a sign of the true importance that the growing Ecuadorian-Iranian ties have had for Ecuador's foreign relations, which—as we will argue later—were until now largely irrelevant.

The Ecuadorian government's answer to the international reaction against Ahmadinejad's visit—and, more generally, to the negotiating of diplomatic ties with Iran—has been to systematically minimize the implications of this fact and a denial that it is sending a message to the United States. The government claims it is strictly an economic move. Ecuador's Deputy Foreign Minister Rafael Paredes told *Vanguardia* magazine in October of 2006 that "there are no intentions of establishing a block of countries to reinforce Iran's position," nor was it in any way "a move against the United States... It is in Ecuador's best interests to have diplomatic relations with all countries." Mr. Paredes interpreted his government's diplomatic bond with Ahmadinejad's government as a "sovereign decision" made by Ecuador, and he pointed out that other Latin American countries maintain trade relationships with Iran as well. "We are interested in Iran because their economy complements ours quite well." Nevertheless, Paredes admits that dealing with Iran creates quite a bit of political chatter. "Diplomatic relations include everything: culture, trade, policy. If trade is an important part of international relations, why should we deny Iran or any other country the possibility of establishing a political dialogue?"[8]

A later statement, this time by Ecuadorian Foreign Minister María Isabel Salvador, clarified the level of importance Ecuador places on its relationship with Iran. Reaffirming Ecuador's sovereignty, the Foreign Minister says that the nation "has the right to engage in diplomatic relations with any other nation, and in March will enter into a trade agreement with Iran. That is what we are interested in, and nothing else." Because the statement sought to disperse purported US concerns over Ecuadorian-Iranian relations, the Foreign Minister added, "We understand that [American civil servants] might be a bit nervous about this, but based on the conversations we've had [with Washington], our relations are open and positive, and that is the most important thing."[9]

Furthermore, in a television interview broadcast on *Teleamazonas*, Salvador explained that "failure to successfully negotiate a Free Trade Agreement with the United States, Ecuador's strategy is developing a new plan" which consists of "innovative trade proposals that will also include such things as political cooperation and support for national social programs." Relatedly, Foreign Minister Salvador adds, "we cannot focus all of our exports towards the United States, and for that reason, we must open ourselves up to other markets, not necessarily to replace the US, but rather to supplement them." Finally, she accepts that Iran "is a nation that frightens many, but we will have offices in other countries as well... In any case, I do not believe that we should be afraid that this trade relationship [with Iran] will lead to some other form of relationship that will have a political impact."[10]

Although Ecuador's position has been to downplay the political significance of its relationship with Iran, the Iranian government has emphasized the political relevance of its new bond with Ecuador as part of the framework for their policy toward Latin America as a whole. In Quito, for example, President Ahmadinejad extended his nation's offer of support to Venezuela, Nicaragua, and Ecuador "to the rest of the nations who feel oppressed by the American government." In addition, he added that "every town and village that feels the need to defend itself can surely count on Iranian aid."[11] Then, referring again to his overall tour of Latin America, Ahmadinejad encouraged the formation of an anti-imperialistic front consisting of left-leaning governments in the region. "An opposition to domination is very strong in Latin America, and the dominant powers are afraid," he declared upon his return to Tehran.[12]

Similarly, Iranian Deputy Foreign Minister Alireza Sheikh Attar, who visited Ecuador in August 2007, reiterated the offers of cooperation in several different areas, and expressed the government's desire to further advance the diplomatic relations between the two countries. Sheikh Attar indicated that Iran was interested in supporting Ecuador in much the same way that it supports Venezuela, which is to say, "so that Ecuador can achieve economic independence. May the entire nation understand that we are offering our support." In particular, Sheikh Attar reminded everyone that since the visit from Iran's chief executive, "our Presidents, on the basis of the similarities of their visions and their political positions [among other things], decided to deepen the bilateral relations between Iran and Ecuador."[13]

What has Actually Happened since Ahmadinejad Visited Quito?

Since Ahmadinejad's visit to Ecuador, little has in fact happened in terms of institutionalizing the emerging diplomatic ties between the two countries. There were three noteworthy events:

- The signing of an agreement to open trade offices in Tehran and Quito on February 28, 2008. Both offices were opened in June of this year, and the Ecuadorian office opened in Iran was the only new trade office opened in the world during the Correa administration.

- The visit to Ecuador by an official Iranian economic delegation, presided by Deputy Foreign Minister Alireza Sheikh Attar, in August 2007. This delegation held meetings with Ecuador's Ministry of Foreign Affairs and Ministry of Petroleum, Energy, and Mines, and representatives from the private sector. The result of this visit was the signing of a "Memorandum of Understanding for the Establishment of a Joint Economic Commission." Also signed were agreements relating to the private sector, and to the exchange of information on construction and petroleum industries. Additionally, the Iranian delegation invited the Ecuadorian Ministers of Petroleum and Agriculture to visit Iran to explore possibilities for cooperating on joint business deals.

- The visit to Iran by 26 Ecuadorian industrialists, presided over by Vice Minister of Trade and Integration Antonio Ruales, in November 2007, with the goal of establishing commercial relations. The businessmen who participated in this visit included flower, tuna, construction, and nutrition industry representatives.

Of the events which took place during that year and a half timeframe, the most significant by far was the signing of the "Memorandum of Understanding" resulting from Sheikh Attar's visit. This memorandum proposed the creation of a Joint Economic Commission, which was reciprocated by Ecuador with their trip to Iran in November 2007.

The document explicitly states that both countries intend not only to promote the expansion of trade between one another, but to also cooperate in developing a number of scientific and technological fields, particularly those of mining, energy, petroleum, information, and communications. In sum, aside from this memorandum and the opening of offices in Quito and Tehran, nothing resulted from extended Ecuadorian-Iranian diplomatic relations. To explain this, one must analyze each country's foreign policy in a broader regional and international context.

Venezuelan and Ecuadorian Foreign Policy and Growing Diplomatic Relations between Ecuador and Iran

As a primary conclusion, we can affirm that institutionalizing diplomatic ties between Ecuador and Iran has been a slow, mostly trade-based process. Overall, nothing—or next to nothing—has happened so far. The establishment of trade offices in both countries doubtlessly represents the beginning of much greater public and private activity and exchange.

On the other hand, while Iranian authorities have mentioned the geopolitical implications of strengthening bilateral relations, the Ecuadorians have sought to downplay politics and highlight economics. It is important to note that President Correa, despite his extroverted demeanor in foreign policy, has only occasionally spoken directly about Ecuadorian—Iranian relations, stating that these new trade relations are advancing because Iran is a complementary market for Ecuador's exportable products. During one of his usual Saturday radio broadcasts, Correa also defended Tehran's right to use atomic energy for peaceful means, despite the fact that the United States sees the possibility of Iran using the technology for military purposes.[14]

Along those same lines, in official documents published on Rafael Correa's foreign policy, diplomatic relations with Iran and other Middle Eastern countries are not mentioned among the government's higher priorities. The chapter on foreign policy in the *National Plan of Development: 2007-2010* dedicates a single sentence to the Middle

East. It states that "the countries of the Middle East offer opportunities for exchange that should be taken advantage of."[15] The political and trade priorities lie in the neighboring countries of Latin America, as well as the United States, Europe, and, to a lesser extent, some Asian nations. There is, however, mention of the importance of maintaining national sovereignty, not only in political and territorial aspects, but also in terms of managing natural resources, biodiversity, and cultural plurality.[16]

In sum, unlike with Venezuela, Bolivia, and Nicaragua, Iran and Ecuador do not have bilateral agreements to cooperate in specific areas like energy, nor has Ecuador received any economic payment or stimulus from Iran. The institutionalization of diplomatic relations between both countries proceeds at an all but imperceptible rate, and—at least on the part of Ecuador's government—it is not being used as a rhetorical gesture or affirmation of sovereignty, or even as a link to some theory of international politics.

In this context, then, the question is why did the government of Ecuador decide to develop its relations with Iran? Quito's argument that trade is the one determining factor of the relationship between the two nations lacks substance when one considers the low volume of exports to Iran, and the scant possibility that these numbers will multiply into significant figures in the next few years. The aforementioned CORPEI study on trade potential between Ecuador and Iran indicates that the possibility of expanding exports of bananas and other fruits, coffee, and flowers does exist. Fish, flour, palm oil, confectionaries, jams, and wood might also be on that list, though they are imported by Iran from other Latin American nations, and would have to be replaced by Ecuador's products.[17] In any case, the opportunity for significant exports to Iran are comparatively small, and would hardly justify such a controversial diplomatic relationship with a government whose ideology is so starkly opposite of Ecuador's "citizens' revolution" government. All this runs contrary to recent declarations by Ecuadorian trade officials in Tehran, who are looking to increase exports to USD $200 million in the next three years.[18]

Furthermore, it is also important to recognize that the Iranian issue has not been used by Ecuador's government to explain its continued calls for national defense, nor has it made any threatening speeches on an international level. On the contrary, Ecuador's position has been to divest its dealings with Iran of all geopolitical connotations and pin them instead on pure and simple economics. However, its defensive position and affirmation of national sovereignty constitute a key piece of its foreign policy.

Setting aside both possibilities for now, we must tightly focus our analysis as a political scope in the context of Ecuadorian-Iranian relations. Our hypothesis is that the Iran-Ecuador relationship cannot be explained in and of itself; rather, it must be viewed as a much more long reaching international dynamic, one which includes other countries, though none more essential than Venezuela. Ecuador's government has maintained a narrow though complex political, economic, and energy relationship with this country within the framework of a clear, ideological similarity between Presidents Chávez and Correa. In other words, from the point of view of Ecuador's government, their diplomatic relationship with Iran can only be understood based on its relationship with Venezuela. Ecuador's government does not have any serious motivations— neither trade opportunities nor the strengthening of national positions—to bring about such a controversial approach to a country that offers little in the way of trade and whose government is at such deep ideological differences with its own. Ecuadorian-Iranian relations are directly correlated to Venezuela, and depend on how close Ecuador wants to be aligned with Chávez's government.

The relationship between Chávez and Correa has certainly been complicated. The Ecuadorian president has gone to great lengths both nationally and internationally to appear aligned with Venezuela. For this reason—despite the empathy and friendship between Chávez and Correa—Ecuador has maintained a cautious distance and a policy of selective convergence with the Venezuelan government instead of complete, unrestrained alignment. In this sense, Ecuador has chosen to adopt simply an observatory status when it comes to issues such as the ALBA Process[19] and Chávez's anti-American and nationalistic rhetoric, and has occasionally gone so far as to take markedly different stances than the Venezuelans. In any case, Ecuador and Venezuela have coincided on energy, military, and political issues, as evidenced by their membership in UNASUR.[20] Furthermore, since the inauguration of President Correa, Ecuador and Venezuela have signed twelve bilateral oil and natural gas agreements with PDVSA[21].

On average, considering Ecuador's lukewarm geopolitical alliance with Venezuela, strong on some occasions and weak on others, Ecuador is able to maintain its image of independence. Early on in Correa's government, the bonds with Venezuela were tightly knit and evident in both the energy and political realms; it was during that juncture that Ahmadinejad visited Quito, beginning the relationship between Ecuador and Iran. Since then, however, Venezuelan-Ecuadorian relations have dissipated, making the issue of Ecuador's relationship with Iran less and less relevant. When the attack on the FARC base led to the death of Raúl Reyes[22], both Venezuela and Ecuador joined in condemning Colombia's military incursion as a violation of Ecuador's sovereignty. However, relations between the two countries returned to their lukewarm status once Ecuador's government announced that it would not become a full member of the ALBA Process, which Iran was involved with from an observational standpoint. This last point may well cool off other issues which affect both Ecuador and Venezuela, including their relationships with Iran.

In conclusion, the case of Iran is part of a lukewarm geopolitical alignment that Ecuador maintains with Venezuela, and as such, it will have some effect on whether the bilateral dynamics between the two South American nations will speed up or slow down. As such, we must take note of the progress (however slow) in diplomatic and trade relations between Ecuador and Iran. Depending on how they measure their relations with Venezuela, Ecuador could either advance or end its relationship with Iran. On the other hand, it would also seem to be the case that for Iran's government, Venezuela is of central importance to its general, hemispheric policy, and Ecuador has a lesser role. As such, we must specifically conclude that, with regard to Ecuadorian-Iranian relations, we have more empty rhetoric and an alarmed international community than concrete steps towards convergence, cooperation, financial and technological assistance, and/or geopolitical alignment.

Notes

1 With thanks to Pamela Cevallos for her enormous contributions.

2 See "Ecuador niega que acercamiento con Irán sea una señal contra EE.UU.", www.elnuevodiario.com.ni. October 16, 2007.

3 "EE.UU. critica lazos de Irán con A. Latina," http://news.bbc.co.uk, May 8, 2008.

4 Joint Declaration between the Islamic Republic of Iran's Minister of Petroleum, Gholamreza Aghazadeh, and Ecuador's Ministry of Petroleum, Energy and Mines, Diego Tamariz Serrano. Ministry of Foreign Relations Archives, Quito, Ecuador.

5 See CORPEI, "Comercio Ecuador-Irán," Quito, 2007, pp. 1-2.

6 See "Ahmadinejad busca amigos en Latinoamérica", www.lanacion.cl/, January 16, 2007.

7 The ties between the governments of Correa and Néstor and Cristina Kirchner are so strong that the Argentine Embassy in Bogotá has acted as the intermediary between Ecuador and Colombia ever since the two Andean nations broke off diplomatic relations in March of this year.

8 See "Ecuador niega que acercamiento con Irán sea una señal contra EEUU", www.el nuevodiario.com.ni, October 16, 2007.

9 See "Planes comerciales con Estados Unidos e Irán", www.hoy.com.ec, January 4, 2008.

10 Ibid.

11 See "Ahmadinejad busca amigos en Latinoamérica," www.lanacion.cl, January 16, 2007.

12 The Iranian President's deepening interest in leftist governments in Latin America comes as a bit of a surprise, considering his own record of implacable repression of leftist groups in Iran. See Kasra Naji, *Ahmadinejad: The Secret History of Radical Iran's Leader.* Berkeley: University of California Press, 2008, pp. 223-224.

13 See "Irán y Ecuador estrechan relaciones", www.eluniverso.com, August 2, 2007.

14 See "Correa anunció que abrirá oficina comercial en Irán en febrero," www.elcomercio.com, January 19, 2008.

15 See Ministerio de Relaciones Exteriores, Comercio e Integración, *Plan Nacional de Desarrollo: 2007-2010, Política Exterior.* Quito, Imprenta Mariscal, 2007, p. 19.

16 Ibid, p. 23.

17 See CORPEI, "Comercio Ecuador-Irán," Quito, 2007, pp. 3-5.

18 See "Autoridades ecuatorianas se presentarán en Irán para abrir oficina comercial, www.elcomercio.com. June 9, 2008.

19 An agreement signed between Venezuela and Cuba in December 2004, which Chávez described as "a flexible model for the integration of Latin America that places social concerns (such as poverty and affordable oil) at the forefront."

20 In English, USAN, or the Union of South American Nations. There, Venezuela and Brazil have proposed a plan for a NATO-like South American Defense Council. Colombia was the only nation not to join, citing potential relations between Venezuela and FARC rebels.

21 The Venezuelan state-owned oil company Petróleos de Venezuela, S.A.

22 Luis Edgar Devia Silva, a.k.a. Raúl Reyes, a high-ranking member of Revolutionary Armed Forces of Colombia (FARC), was killed by the Colombian military during an operation which carried them a few miles over the border and into Ecuador.

Biographies of Contributors

Cynthia J. Arnson is director of the Latin American Program at the Woodrow Wilson International Center for Scholars. She is editor of *Comparative Peace Processes in Latin America* (Stanford University Press, 1999), co-editor (with I. William Zartman) of *Rethinking the Economics of War: The Intersection of Need, Creed, and Greed* (The Johns Hopkins University Press, 2005), and author of *Crossroads: Congress, the President, and Central America, 1976-1993* (2d ed., Penn State Press, 1993). Arnson served as associate director of the Americas division of Human Rights Watch/Americas from 1990-1994. She served as an assistant professor of international relations at American University's School of International Service 1989-1991, and as a foreign policy aide in the House of Representatives during the Carter and Reagan administrations.

Elodie Brun is a doctoral candidate in political science at the Institut d'Études Politiques (Sciences Po) in Paris, studying South-South relations between Latin America and Africa, Asia, and the Middle East. Her previous research focuses on international relations between the Perso-Arabic and South American countries, particularly Egypt, Iran, Brazil, and Venezuela. She is the author of *Les relations entre l'Amérique du Sud et le Moyen-Orient. Un exemple de relance Sud-Sud* (Paris: L'Harmattan, 2008), among other publications.

Haleh Esfandiari, the director of the Middle East Program at the Woodrow Wilson International Center for Scholars, has had a rich and varied career. In her native Iran, she was a journalist, served as deputy secretary general of the Women's Organization of Iran, and was the deputy director of a cultural foundation where she was responsible for the activities of several museums and art and cultural centers. She taught Persian language and literature at Oxford University and Princeton University. Dr. Esfandiari is the author and editor of a number of books and articles. She is the recipient of a number of awards, including one named after her by a group of Middle Eastern women entrepreneurs in

2008. Her memoir, *My Prison, My Home*, based on Esfandiari's arrest by the Iranian security authorities in 2007, after which she spent 105 days in solitary confinement in Tehran's Evin Prison, was published in September 2009.

Douglas Farah is the president of IBI Consultants and a Senior Fellow at the International Assessment and Strategy Center. He is a national security consultant and analyst. He was a foreign correspondent and investigative reporter for the Washington Post and other publications, extensively covering Latin America, West Africa, and the Caribbean. He has investigated drug wars, drug trafficking, organized crime, radical Islamic groups, and terror finance. He is the author of *Blood from Stones: The Secret Financial Network of Terror* (2004) and with Stephen Braun, *Merchant of Death: money, guns, planes, and the man who makes war possible* (2007). He graduated with honors from the University of Kansas, earning a B.A. in Latin American Studies and a B.S. in Journalism.

Farideh Farhi is currently an independent scholar and Affiliate Graduate Faculty and Lecturer at the University of Hawai'i at Manoa. She has taught comparative politics at the University of Colorado at Boulder, University of Hawai'i at Manoa, University of Tehran, and Shahid Beheshti University, Tehran. She was a Public Policy Scholar at the Woodrow Wilson International Center for Scholars where she conducted research on the roots and nature of political competition in Iran. Her publications include *States and Urban-Based Revolutions in Iran and Nicaragua* (University of Illinois Press, 1990) as well as numerous articles and book chapters on comparative analysis of revolutions and Iranian politics and foreign policy.

Gustavo Fernández served as Bolivia's Minister of Foreign Affairs under three administrations, and has held posts as Minister of the Presidency, Ambassador to Brazil, General Consul in Chile, and Secretary of Integration. A lawyer by training, he has held a number of posts in international organizations, including chief of the OAS Electoral Mission in Nicaragua in 2006, as well as consultancies on development and integration issues with the Andean Development Corporation, the United

Nations Development Program, and the United Nations Economic Commission for Latin America and the Caribbean. Among his recent publications is *Bolivia en el laberinto de la globalización*

Félix Maradiaga co-founded Nicaragua's Ministry of Defense and served as the youngest-ever Secretary General of the Ministry of Defense. Subsequently, he co-founded the Civil Society Leadership Institute (CSLI), an organization dedicated to fostering civic engagement and strengthening democracy and the rule of law in Nicaragua. He is currently a senior researcher at the Institute of Strategic Studies and Public Policy (*Instituto de Estudios Estratégicos y Políticas Públicas,* IEEPP) and a Yale World Fellow at Yale University. He holds a B.A. Summa Cum Laude in Political Science from the University of Mobile (Alabama) and a Masters with honors in Public Administration from Harvard University.

Javier Meléndez is the executive director of the non-governmental Institute of Strategic Studies and Public Policies (IEEPP) in Managua, Nicaragua. For more than twelve years, Meléndez has conducted research on a broad range of defense and security issues, including small arms transfers, as well as on democratic governance and transparency. He also focuses on matters concerning security, modernization of political parties, and poverty reduction from the political and institutional spheres.

Hugo Alconada Mon is the former Washington correspondent and U.S. Bureau Chief of the Argentine newspaper *La Nacion*. He is a graduate of the Law School of the University of La Plata, Argentina, and earned his Master's degree summa cum laude in Political Communication from the University of Navarre, Spain. He is co-author of *Prensa y Congreso* (2002), and has published articles in regional and national media in the United States, Spain, Mexico, Brazil, Colombia, Peru, Uruguay, and Argentina. The winner of scholarships and grants from the United Nations, the Konrad Adenauer Foundation, and the Salzburg Seminar, as well as the top Argentine Award for Journalism (from ADEPA), he has taught in the Universidad Católica de Argentina (UCA) and his alma mater, the Universidad de La Plata. He has also been a visiting scholar at the University of Missouri School of Journalism.

César Montúfar is a professor at the Universidad Andina Simón Bolívar in Quito, Ecuador, and executive director of the Centro Andino de Estudios Internacionales. His areas of expertise include Ecuadoran and Latin American politics, international development, and international security. He holds a Ph.D. in political science from the New School of Social Research, where he won an award for the best doctoral dissertation by a foreign student. He is the author of *Gobernabilidad y Participación* (2004) and *Hacia una teoría de la asistencia internacional del desarrollo* (2002), among other publications.

Adam Stubits is program associate for the Wilson Center's Latin American Program. He received his B.A. in Political Science and M.P.A with an emphasis in international organizations from The American University. His research interests include citizen security in Latin America, informal international organizations and the role of public administration in development. Prior to coming to the Wilson Center, he was a special assistant for International Accounts with the Corporate Executive Board and before that a Development Officer with Partners of the Americas.